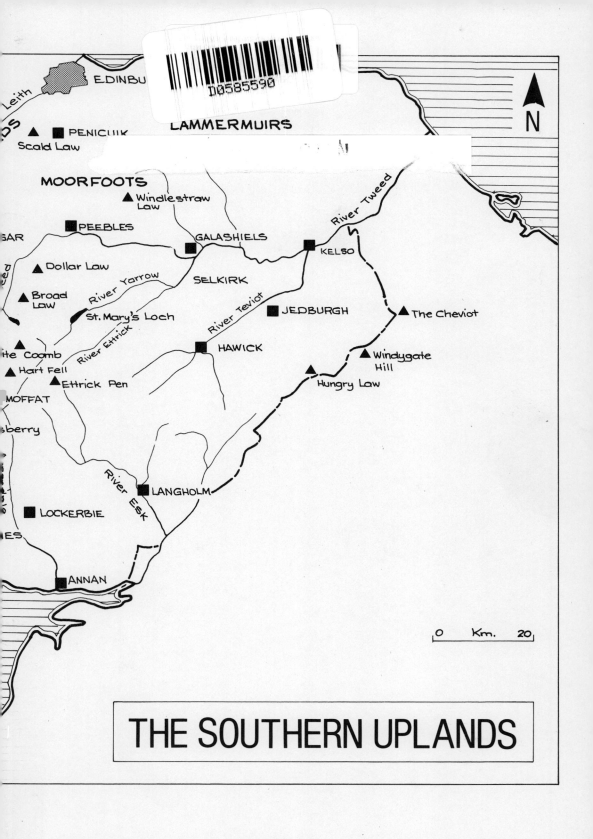

Leith
EDINBU
LAMMERMUIRS

▲ ■ PENICUIK
Scald Law

MOORFOOTS

▲ Windlestraw
Law

■ PEEBLES

GAR

GALASHIELS
■

River Tweed

■ KELSO

▲ Dollar Law

SELKIRK

River Yarrow

▲ Broad
Law

St. Mary's Loch

River Teviot

■ JEDBURGH

▲ The Cheviot

River Ettrick

te Coomb

■ HAWICK

▲ Windygate
Hill

▲ Hart Fell

▲ Ettrick Pen

Hungry Law

MOFFAT

sberry

River Esk

■ LANGHOLM

■ LOCKERBIE

ES

■ ANNAN

0    Km.    20

# THE SOUTHERN UPLANDS

Scottish Mountaineering Club
District Guidebooks

# THE SOUTHERN UPLANDS

Series Editor: D J BENNET

Published by
The Scottish Mountaineering Trust

# THE
# SOUTHERN UPLANDS

## Ken Andrew

Scottish Mountaineering Club District Guidebook

PUBLISHED BY THE SCOTTISH MOUNTAINEERING TRUST: 1992
© THE SCOTTISH MOUNTAINEERING CLUB

First Edition (Andrew and Thrippleton) 1972
Reprinted 1983
Second Edition 1992

British Library Cataloguing in Publication Data
Andrew, Ken
Southern Uplands. - 2nd Rev. Ed. - (Scottish
Mountaineering Club District Guides Series)
I. Title II. Thrippleton A.A.
III. Series
796.51094137

ISBN 0-907521-38-X

Illustrations
Front cover: Taberon Law from Stanhope in the Tweed Valley  *K.M.Andrew*
Back cover: Looking from Craigencolon to Loch Doon *K.M.Andrew*

Book design by Donald Bennet
Maps drawn by Jim Renny
Production by Peter Hodgkiss
Typeset by Westec, North Connel
Colour separations by Par Graphics, Kirkcaldy
Printed by Pillans and Wilson, Edinburgh
Bound by Hunter and Foulis, Edinburgh

Distributed by Cordee, 3a DeMontfort Street, Leicester, LE1 7HD

# CONTENTS

# ILLUSTRATIONS

*Uncredited illustrations by the author*

# FOREWORD

The Southern Uplands are the least known hills of Scotland. The higher mountains of the Highlands and Islands are much more popular for their greater variety and outstanding scenic qualities. There are no hills in the south which can compete with the best in the north. Private cars on modern roads and today's work patterns allow many to gain considerable experience of northern hills in a relatively short time, but the constant urge to explore new territory, whether on Munros, Corbetts, rock walls or hill paths can soon lead to a jaded sense of sufficiency in today's dedicated travellers if they do not seek contrasting pleasures.

The Southern Uplands can offer these pleasures. Though lowly and less spectacular by comparison, they offer surprises and delights just as the northern hills do. A knowledge of Scotland is far from complete without considerable experience of the hills in the south. A vast area stretches across the Southern Uplands offering great variety of scenery and adventure. As the northern hills and roads become more and more congested, so the Southern Uplands will surely become the great discovery of the next decade.

# THE CLIMBER AND THE MOUNTAIN ENVIRONMENT

With increasing numbers of walkers and climbers going to the Scottish hills, it is important that all of us who do so should recognise our responsibilities to those who live and work among the hills and glens, to our fellow climbers and to the mountain environment in which we find our pleasure and recreation.

The Scottish Mountaineering Club and Trust, who jointly produce this and other guidebooks, wish to impress on all who avail themselves of the information in these books that it is essential at all times to consider the sporting and proprietory rights of landowners and farmers. The description of a climbing, walking or skiing route in any of these books does not imply that a right of way exists, and it is the responsibility of all climbers to ascertain the position before setting out. In cases of doubt it is always best to enquire locally.

During the stalking and shooting seasons in particular, much harm can be done in deer forests and on grouse moors by people walking through them. Normally the deer stalking season is from 1st July to 20th October, when stag shooting ends. Hinds may continue to be culled until 15th February. The grouse shooting season is from 12th August until 10th December. These are not merely sporting activities, but are essential for the economy of many Highland estates. During these seasons, therefore, especial care should be taken to consult the local landowner, factor or keeper before taking to the hills.

Climbers and hillwalkers are recommended to consult the book *Heading for the Scottish Hills,* published by the Scottish Mountaineering Trust on behalf of the Mountaineering Council of Scotland and the Scottish Landowners Federation, which gives the names and addresses of factors and keepers who may be contacted for information regarding access to the hills.

It is also important to avoid disturbance to sheep, particularly during the lambing season between March and May. Dogs should not be taken onto the hills at this time, and at all times should be kept under close control.

Always try to follow a path or track through cultivated land and forests, and avoid causing damage to fences, dykes and gates by climbing over them carelessly. Do not leave litter anywhere, but take it down from the hill in your rucksack.

The increasing number of walkers and climbers on the hills is leading to increased, and in some cases very unsightly erosion of footpaths and hillsides. Some of the revenue from the sale of this and other SMC guidebooks is used by the Trust to assist financially the work being carried out to repair and maintain hill paths in Scotland. However, it is important for all of us to recognise our responsibility to minimise the erosive effect of our passage over the hills so that the enjoyment of future climbers shall not be spoiled by landscape damage caused by ourselves.

As a general rule, where a path exists walkers should follow it and even where it is wet and muddy should avoid walking along its edges, the effect of which is to extend erosion sideways. Do not take short-cuts at the corners of zigzag paths. Remember that the worst effects of erosion are likely to be caused during or soon after prolonged wet weather when the ground is soft and waterlogged. A route on a stony or rocky hillside is likely to cause less erosion than on a grassy one at such times.

Although the use of bicycles can often be very helpful for reaching remote hills and crags, the erosion damage that can be caused by them when used 'off road' on soft footpaths and open hillsides is such that their use on such terrain must cause concern. It is the editorial policy of the Scottish Mountaineering Club that the use of bicycles in hill country may be recommended on hard roads such as forest roads or private roads following rights of way, but is not recommended on footpaths and open hillsides where the environmental damage that they cause may be considerable. Readers are asked to bear these points in mind, particularly in conditions when the ground is wet and soft after rain.

The proliferation of cairns on the hills detracts from the feeling of wildness, and may be confusing rather than helpful as regards route-finding. The indiscriminate building of cairns on the hills is therefore to be discouraged.

Climbers are reminded that they should not drive along private estate roads without permission, and when parking their cars should avoid blocking access to private roads and land, and should avoid causing any hazard to other road users.

Finally, the Scottish Mountaineering Club and the Scottish Mountaineering Trust can accept no liability for damage to property nor for personal injury resulting from the use of any route described in their publications.

*Talla Linnfoots and the Games Hope Burn from Talla Cleuch Head*

# Introduction

It is a convenient generalisation to divide Scotland into the three regions of Highlands and Islands, Central Lowlands, and Southern Uplands, but the boundary between these is not always as obvious as is supposed.

A northern boundary of the Southern Uplands can be placed along a fault line running roughly from Girvan to Dunbar with the Central Lowlands lying in a rift valley to the north. The frontier can be seen clearly in Ayrshire and East Lothian, but in the centre of the country the fault line and the edge of the high ground part company. Here the dividing line in the landscape detours northwards to enclose Tinto Hill and the Pentlands, thus upsetting the simplicity of the frontier. At the north-western extremity of the Central Lowlands the hills south of the Clyde estuary rise to over 500m and cannot be ignored in a book dealing with the uplands of Southern Scotland.

To the south of the Southern Uplands, the plains around Annan and the lower Tweed are clear boundaries of the hill zones, but again, in the centre of the country, the hills spill over a frontier dividing Scotland politically from England. The Cheviot Hills formed a much fought-over frontier in our turbulent past, but today's emancipated walkers can enjoy high-level forays into England without pikes, pickets or passports. Accordingly, this book has included uplands which might be claimed for the Central Lowlands or which stretch over a frontier into another country.

The structure of the Southern Uplands has determined much of its history, its social organisation, and the land use that we see today. Hill ranges and river valleys influenced invaders, settlers, traders and farmers. Early travellers made their ways through the hills by trial and error. In prehistoric times the valleys and lower hill slopes must have been densely wooded, but gradually pathways were developed by parties hunting, trading or marauding. These pathways were further developed by Roman invaders who also stamped their own routes across the map with a direct and logical precision which has to be admired by today's hill-tribes and gangrels.

The most direct route through the Southern Uplands today uses the Annan and Clyde valleys and, significantly, is partly on the line of a Roman road. South to north communications are in general much simpler than east to west routes. As an illustration, a motorist driving between Ayr and Berwick should find it much quicker to go the indirect way round by East Kilbride, the M8, and the Edinburgh bypass than to head directly for Peebles and Kelso on a route which appears to be much shorter.

The hill and river barriers of Southern Scotland have isolated cultures from each other so that rugby and common ridings are great enthusiasms in the east but not in the west. Climate also draws a divide across the country with different farming methods practised between the wetter grasslands of the west and drier seed-beds of the east, though soil-types, altitude and exposure add great variations.

Forestry has had a dramatic impact on many parts of Southern Scotland since the 1960s. A monotonous monocultural spread of spruce has added a dark green gloom to many a valley, effectively ending the right to roam. In some areas the foresters have not known when to stop, and have blighted the scenery and offended their allies. In other areas, a happier mix of larch, hardwoods and open spaces has enhanced the landscape, bringing seasonal contrasts to sensitively developed pan-oramas. The Border Forest Park and the Galloway Forest Park encourage visitors and have developed information centres, forest walks, drives and cycle routes, camp sites and other facilities, while a number of individual forests also provide visitor attractions. Forestry policy continues to alter under government pressure and walkers need to play a constructive part in the debate.

Hillwalkers are less numerous in the Southern Uplands than in the Highlands and should meet fewer problems of access. The Uplands have fewer red deer to control or exploit than the Highlands, though grouse moors are just as jealously preserved. Conflicts are most likely to arise with farmers at lambing time when sheep are all too easily disturbed and distressed by intruders. Walkers need to show extra consideration at this time of year to maintain the good relationship necessary to preserve the freedom of the hills.

## DYKES AND FENCES

Dry stone walls, often in ruinous condition, can be found running along a number of ridges in the Southern Uplands. These often marked parish or county boundaries in the past and may well be district or regional boundaries today. They can be useful guides in mist. There are few dykers in business to maintain these walls today and wire fences are now the norm. One or more strands of barbed wire can make crossing these troublesome. Deer fences around forestry can be higher and harder to climb.

Electric fences are now common in parts of the Southern Uplands and can be recognised by the rubber insulators they carry on the upright posts. Most of the fences can deliver only a fairly minor shock if touched, but several fences under Cairnsgarroch in Galloway carry 5000 volts and can give a very painful jolt. The consequences of becoming entangled in such a fence are horrifying.

Some of the earliest electric fences in the Uplands have proved difficult to maintain and it is impossible to forecast the hazards which may lie ahead. Walkers should always use gates if available, and leave these, walls and fences as they find them, so that fortifications are not strengthened for their next visit. Where access to walkers is unreasonably restricted, counter-measures may be required to preserve traditional routes.

## MILITARY USE OF THE HILLS

The Ministry of Defence has shown great interest in Southern Scotland in recent years and will probably continue to do so in response to criticism regarding its activities in England and elsewhere. Low-flying aircraft are common weekday terrors which puncture the walker's bliss. In the Pentlands and the Eildons exclusion zones debar walkers from live-firing shooting areas, while Galloway has seen a number of massive military exercises involving thousands of personnel, causing unrepaired damage and leaving a mess of litter. Walkers need to be outspoken to defend their interests.

## MAPS

The 1:50,000 Ordnance Survey maps of the Landranger series are recommended for use with this guide as they provide adequate detail for hill-walks and cover more distance than most walkers will complete in a day. Where large areas of forest are encountered, the 1:25,000 Ordnance Survey maps of the Pathfinder series are more useful as they depict firebreaks. These maps also include more place-names and items of topographical interest, but can be inconvenient when three or four sheets are needed on one walk. About a dozen Landranger series maps will cover most of the ground in the south of Scotland, but about eight times more Pathfinder series maps will be required for the same area at considerably more expense.

Bartholomew 1:100,000 Leisure maps are useful for general travel and for gaining an overall impression of hill ranges, but these maps are not detailed enough for route-finding in forests. Their coloured height intervals of 100 metres can also fail to warn of much tedious up and down work where a route appears to be straight-forward. The series is not complete for the Southern Uplands.

Two maps especially published by HMSO for the Countryside Commission for Scotland on a scale of 1:50,000 show the route of the Southern Upland Way - and numerous Donalds besides. Bartholomew also issue a useful walkers' map of the Pentlands while Harvey maps cover the major ranges of Galloway and the main Cheviot Hills. Heights shown in this guide are taken from the latest maps available whether in the Landranger or Pathfinder series.

## CORBETTS AND DONALDS

Hills of 2000 feet and above in the Scottish Lowlands are known as Donalds, after Percy Donald who listed them in height order, following on the lists by Sir Hugh Munro and J.Rooke Corbett of Scottish hills 3000 feet and above (Munros), and 2500-2999 feet (Corbetts). The three lists are published in one volume titled *Munro's Tables* by the Scottish Mountaineering Trust. In metric terms Munros start at 914m, Corbetts at 762m, and Donalds at 610m.

There are seven Corbetts but no Munros in the Southern Uplands. These seven Corbetts also rank among eighty two Donalds in the Southern Uplands in the revised

Donald's Tables, which also list forty seven subsidiary Donald tops, plus six heights in the Cheviots on the English side of the border which rise to 2000 feet or more.

## TRANSPORT

Public transport is inadequate for many communities in the south of Scotland and walkers have a big problem if they do not have a vehicle. Although several rail routes run through the Southern Uplands, there are no stations open on them which are near the main hill ranges. One or two stations can be used at the start or end of a long lineal cross-country route, but none of them are any help for a normal hill-walk save in the area between Ardrossan and Greenock where the train can offer an advantage. Bus deregulation has brought a scramble by operators for the more profitable urban routes, but has served country areas badly. Some companies are now reluctant to publish timetables lest competitors poach their passengers!

The situation is very unstable and up-to-date information on routes and times should be sought from companies before journeys are undertaken.

## ACCOMMODATION

The population of the south of Scotland is fairly thinly but widely spread in small towns, villages and smaller settlements. Accommodation available to travellers varies from large and small hotels, guest houses, farm houses, and bed and breakfast premises to self-catering establishments and camping and caravan sites.

A number of forests welcome visitors and have camping and caravan sites. Campers should seek permission from landowners before camping outside official sites, but walkers coming off the hills late in the evening are unlikely to find anyone around to complain if they camp discreetly in upper valleys. The streams in many glens are used as water supplies for farms and cottages or are collected in reservoirs to be piped to distant towns. Camps should not be set up in such catchment areas and it is important that no water supply is polluted.

Many dwellings once inhabited by shepherds and their families have now been abandoned. The sites may remain only as heaps of stones, as derelict ruins, or as wind and watertight but vacant buildings which may or may not be locked. Several habitable buildings are open for passers-by to use freely. The Mountain Bothies Association has played a leading role in repairing several remote bothies and has encouraged landowners by the responsible attitude of its members to allow these empty buildings to be used as shelters by passing walkers. Those availing themselves of this privilege should leave the buildings as good as when they find them and should carry home their litter.

Details are given at the start of each chapter of hotel accommodation, bothies available and camping sites. Local tourist boards publish fuller lists of accommodation and local information centres can supply these along with Scottish Tourist Board publications.

# WEATHER

Westerly winds dominate the weather of the Southern Uplands. The weather pattern is similar to that of the Scottish Highlands, though lower altitudes and more southerly latitudes bring less severe conditions. Precipitation is greatest along the high ground nearest to the west coast, and slackens off eastwards where there is more chance of the clouds breaking and the sun shining through. Low ground near the west coast also enjoys more sun and less precipitation than high ground farther inland. Winds from an easterly direction can reverse this pattern temporarily and bring some precipitation to the easterly ranges while westerly hills enjoy sun.

East Lothian, Berwickshire and the Solway coast are the sunniest places in the south of Scotland while sunshine figures decrease as the ground rises inland. Average annual rainfall of around 200cm on the Galloway Hills decreases to around 100cm on the Cheviots and Lammermuirs. Coastal haar, or sea fog, can affect the east coast during the summer months as warm air condenses over a cold sea. This can drift far enough inland to spoil a day on eastern ranges, but such mists may break up as the day progresses. The late winter, spring, and early summer months tend to be the driest and sunniest in the Southern Uplands and often bring the best visibility. Winds from the south and east tend to bring hazy conditions while winds from the west or north-west often bring excellent visibility.

The higher temperatures of the summer months bring out the flies and midges, which, in a greener and often hazier landscape, seriously detract from the appeal of the outdoors. Autumn is the most colourful time of the year when leaves and grasses can be spectacular. This is the shortest season of the year though, and can be ruined by Atlantic depressions whirling the leaves away and obscuring the sun.

Snowfall is very unpredictable. Heavy falls can occur at any time between November and March while showers can blanket the ground in the autumn or spring months. Years of little snow and few frosts can be followed by severe periods, but past records are not complete enough to build patterns on.

# GEOLOGY

The sweeping curves of the Southern Upland hills, with their relatively few outcrops, suggest a simple and uniform rock structure underlying the rather mon-otonous moorland vegetation. The impression is reinforced by the uniform heights of many of the hills. From a high central viewpoint the prospect to east and west is over ranges of hills of similar form and altitude with scarcely a peaked point or rocky edge in sight.

This can lead the viewer to fall into the trap of concluding that the region has evolved from a huge tableland built up of level layers of strata, which has been breached at numerous places, and has since had its rough edges ground down by erosive forces to the smooth outlines evident today.

While this impression is not totally false, the picture is very much more complicated. For a start, the strata is highly contorted, and underneath a thinly vegetated
skin the layers of rock can surface at steeply inclined, or even vertical angles. The
landscape has evolved through complex processes which are not yet fully under-
stood, and may never be. Many of the clues needed for solving the mysteries are
missing, swept away long before humans appeared on the scene.

Nearly all of the uplands have been formed from sedimentary rocks, but a
number of igneous intrusions have made a great impact on the landscape. Much of
the surface of the past has simply disappeared - redistributed by ice, water and
weather - and now overlies or is buried under other areas.

## Ordovician and Silurian

The oldest sedimentary rocks evident in the Southern Uplands are of the Ordovician
system of Lower Palaeozoic age. These lie in a broad band stretching from Portpatrick to the Lammermuirs along the northern edge of the Southern Uplands. A
broader band of Silurian rocks lies to the south and also follows this south-west to
north-east trend between the Mull of Galloway and St Abb's Head.

The two systems are composed of thin bands of sediments which were laid down
in seas and compressed under their own weight and that of the water into shales,
greywackes, mudstones and conglomerates. Uplifting of the land or lowering of the
waters, possibly on numerous occasions, caused these rocks to become subject to
erosion in its many forms.

Intense compression during the Caledonian mountain-building period led to the
level strata becoming folded in waves like a concertina. As great anticlines built up,
some cracked under stress allowing the erosive forces access to their rough edges.
So began the slow process of smoothing out the landscape again. Before that stage
could be reached further submersion and deposition of sediments took place filling
in the hollows.

The coastlines provide the best clues to this basic structure of the Southern
Uplands, along the west-facing cliffs of Galloway or the North Sea cliffs of Berwickshire and East Lothian. Here, where the vegetation cannot hold a grip on the
high-angled strata, under the constant attack of the waves, salt spray and normal
aerial forces of erosion, the bands of sediments are exposed and can be followed as
they twist and fold from the edges of the sea to the top of the cliffs, in sweeping
arches, zigzags, and thin vertical bands. Inland these highly-tilted and folded layers
of strata are mainly hidden under a surface layer of vegetation and glacial debris.
Where the rocks are exposed they quickly break down at an even rate to smaller and
smaller stones and grits which are blown away or are colonised by vegetation again.

The Ordovician and Silurian scenery of the Southern Uplands is undramatic in
the main, with hills of rolling outlines and few crags or exposures of rock. Being
lower than many Highland hills they experience a less severe climate and longer
growing season, so that grasses and heather can flourish on upland ridges and totally
envelop some hills.

## Old Red Sandstone and Carboniferous

Further deposition of sediments occurred in Southern Scotland during Old Red Sandstone times, accompanying more earth movements and volcanic activity which continued into the Carboniferous Period. The sediments were deposited this time on the upended layers of Lower Palaeozoic rocks, but have been mostly cleaned away again by erosion. They have survived in the Pentlands and can be studied at Siccar Point on the East Lothian coast where a marked unconformity exists between the Old Red Sandstone and underlying Silurian strata. The striking distiction between the red and grey bands of rock on this coastline is a feature of the view from Fast Castle Head.

Possibly exploiting lines of weakness in the intensely folded Ordovician and Silurian systems, intrusions of volcanic material welled up at various points during this period. These are represented most dramatically today by the granite ranges of Galloway. The Dungeon Range, south of Loch Doon, holds the wildest scenery of Southern Scotland, while Cairnsmore of Fleet and Criffel are rough and rugged areas disguised from a distance by the smooth outlines of their summits. Considerable baking occurred in the sediments around the intrusions near Loch Doon and is visible on the higher hills of Galloway which form a metamorphic aureole around the central granite cauldron. The bright red colouring of the Old Red Sandstone landscape is also a feature of parts of the Lammermuirs, the Leader Water Valley south of Lauder and the Rule Water Valley near Jedburgh.

Another metamorphic aureole surrounds the granite intrusion of The Cheviot and forms its most dramatic scenery where a tough belt of rock weathers slowly at Bizzle Crags, West Hill over the Hen Hole, and The Schil, to compensate for the disappointingly dull granite core. Lava flows from the Carboniferous Age have left us the attractive peaked landscape of the Borders Country where Rubers Law, Skelfhill Pen, Maiden Paps, the Dirrington Laws and other hills are mini-mountains in form. The triple-peaked Eildons are thought to be a composite laccolith exposed by the erosion of the overlying rocks. The outlying Tinto Hill and Traprain Law are also considered to be laccoliths. The latter's scenic impact on the Lothian Plain is remarkable for a hill of only 200m. A similar impact is made by other volcanic midgets such as North Berwick Law and Arthur's Seat further north and west.

The influence of geology on the landscape and vegetation is perhaps best illustrated in the Pentlands when walking west from the lavas of the higher hills to the Old Red Sandstone of East Cairn Hill.

## New Red Sandstone

Red Permian exposures are striking features of the scenery of Nithsdale, Annandale and the River Ayr's gorge at Ballochmyle, but are not found on the high hills of the Southern Uplands.

## Pleistocene

The southern landscapes of Scotland were extensively remodelled during the ice ages. Ice caps were probably centred in Galloway and the Tweedsmuir Hills. The

*The Maiden Paps from Scaw'd Law*

glaciated scenery of Galloway is particularly striking, and massive boulders dumped by the ice stud the upper grassy slopes of Merrick around the highest summit in the Southern Uplands.

The easily destroyed rocks of the Southern Uplands have not allowed corrie formations to develop so well as in the Highlands, but crescent-shaped scoops have eaten into some such as the Tweedsmuir Hills while a powerful stream of ice has excavated a deep trench for the Moffat Water, leaving a spectacular hanging valley at the Grey Mare's Tail.

Ice moving northwards from the Southern Uplands encountered stronger streams of ice pushing southwards out of the Scottish Highlands and was diverted to east and west or joined the general surge towards the south. The streams of ice forced eastwards along the northern edge of the Southern Uplands have produced a series of remarkable melt-water channels around the Lammermuirs, which give that range a unique quality which is generally overlooked by those obsessed with summits.

Heavy accumulations of snow and ice on high ground compressed the land surface. As the snow and ice melted in warmer periods this weight was removed and the ground was able to expand again. Sea-levels adjusted themselves in accord

*Erratic boulders near the summit of Merrick*

with these changes and valley floors became transit routes for glaciers, meltwater and rock detritus from the hills. Where the valleys were unable to cope with the seaward momentum the retaining walls were breached and new routes instigated by invincible streams.

The watershed of the Southern Uplands follows the south-west to north-east trend of the hill country, sending the Rivers Clyde, Irvine, Ayr, Doon, Girvan and Stinchar north and west to the Firth of Clyde, and the Rivers Cree, Dee, Nith, Annan and Esk south and east to the Solway Firth. The River Tweed starts off in a northwards direction flowing roughly parallel to the Clyde before swinging away eastwards in the opposite direction to the North Sea. The Biggar Gap between the two rivers suggests that one of them may once have used it.

The River Nith has an extraordinary journey. It starts off on a northerly course, virtually escaping from the Southern Uplands, then changes direction to the east and plunges back into the hills through the Sanquhar Gap to fight its way south to the Solway Firth.

The drainage pattern of the Southern Uplands has obviously been influenced by land formations which no longer exist, while glaciation has been a finishing tool in modelling the present landscape.

# CHAPTER 1

# The Eastern Cheviot Hills

| | | |
|---|---|---|
| **The Schil** | 601m | 870 223 |
| **The Cheviot** | 815m | 909 205 |
| **Cushat Law** | 615m | 928 138 |
| **Bloodybush Edge** | 610m | 902 144 |
| **Comb Fell** | 652m | 924 187 |
| **Hedgehope Hill** | 714m | 944 198 |
| **Windy Gyle** | 619m | 855 152 |
| **Brownhart Law** | 507m | 788 094 |
| **Hungry Law** | 501m | 747 061 |

Scotland shares this group of hills with England. The frontier follows the high ground along the lengthy chain of the Cheviots in a rough L-shape from the River Tweed and Merse of Berwickshire between the North Sea and Carter Bar on the A68. Because of this L-shape alignment, the division between the two countries runs in a north-south direction for a considerable distance. Kinks in the chain even cause Scotland to lie to the south of England in several places.

The hills of this chapter, and some of those in the next, run across one of the narrowest parts of Britain, stretching from the Solway Firth to the Northumbrian coast. The coastal plains carry the main north-south road and rail routes, leaving the central ground largely undeveloped. Wars between the two countries in the past made this a particularly troublesome area to control, always subject to invasion and counter-invasion by armies and bands of rievers. Various hill paths between the two countries are a legacy of these times, though some are overgrown now through lack of use, and some are in danger of becoming lost in afforestation or by the activities of the Ministry of Defence who own a large area between the rivers Rede and Coquet and use it as an artillery and infantry training area. When red flags or lamps are displayed on the boundaries do not enter this area or you could be killed.

Most of the major summits in this chapter lie on the English side of the border, but hillwalkers are notoriously irreverent concerning boundaries and many interesting expeditions can be made from the Scottish side. No attempt has been made to describe all the routes into the Cheviots from England as that is outwith the scope of this book.

## ACCESS
The A68 from Jedburgh to Carter Bar and Otterburn. The A698 from north of Jedburgh to Cornhill-on-Tweed. The A697 from Cornhill-on-Tweed to Morpeth. From the A698, the B6401, B6436, B6352 and B6396 head eastwards to the valleys of the Kale and Bowmont Waters. Morebattle, Town Yetholm and Kirk Yetholm are route centres here and send off other minor roads into the hills. From the A697, the B6351 and other minor roads offer routes from England into the hills by the College, Harthope and Breamish valleys. Another route from England leaves the B6341 and goes up Coquetdale to Chew Green near the Border. When red flags are not flying, drivers may be allowed to continue across the military range to the A68 on the modern road which follows the line of Gamel's Path and Dere Street.

## TRANSPORT
*Bus:* Edinburgh to Jedburgh, Otterburn and Newcastle;
Berwick to Wooler; daily.
Hawick to Bonchester Bridge; Monday to Saturday.
Jedburgh to Chesters; schooldays and Saturday.
Hawick to Chesters; Wednesday, Thursday and Saturday.
Kelso to Morebattle and Kirk Yetholm; daily.
Jedburgh to Oxnam and Upper Hindhope; schooldays.
Newcastle to Rothbury; daily.

*Postbus:* Rothbury to Alwinton; Monday to Saturday.
Wooler to Kirknewton, Hethpool and Goldscleugh; Monday to Saturday.

## ACCOMMODATION
Hotels at Coldstream, Cornhill-on-Tweed, Jedburgh, Kelso, Hawick, Kirk Yetholm, Bonchester Bridge, Morebattle, Wooler and Rothbury.
Youth hostels at Kirk Yetholm, Wooler, Bellingham and Byrness.
Camp and caravan sites at Bonchester Bridge, Jedburgh, Hawick, Town Yetholm, and River Breamish.
Bothies at Auchope Rig (879 201) and Lamb Hill (804 129).

## MAPS
Ordnance Survey 1:50,000, Sheets 74, 75, 80 and 81
Bartholomew 1:100,000, The Borders
Harvey 1:40,000, The Eastern Cheviots
                    The Western Cheviots

Cheviot granite has not created distinctive land-forms like the Arran hills or Cairngorms and is largely concealed under a blanket of damp and monotonous moorland cover. The area has many surprises to offer though and well rewards exploration.

The English sector of the Cheviots lies within the Northumberland National Park. The park has information centres at Ingram and Rothbury and information points at Harbottle Post Office and the Border Reiver in Otterburn.

In 1980, a public inquiry was held into an appeal by the Atomic Energy Authority against the refusal by Northumberland County Council to grant planning consent for test drilling in connection with nuclear waste disposal at Usway and Chillingham

*The Schil*

forests on the south and east sides of the Cheviot range. The inquiry was overtaken by a national rethink on this contentious issue and the problem remains to be faced in the future.

## THE HILLS

### The Schil (601m)

An easy rock scramble is required to reach the summit of this hill, for unlike other Cheviots it has a very distinctive tor shape.

The road south from Town Yetholm leads up the Bowmont Water to Sourhope, giving close access to the south-west ridge of the hill past Auchope. If approaching from Kirk Yetholm, follow the road south-east to the Halter Burn where cars drive to near Burnhead. A track past Old Halterburnhead leads to a col between The Curr and Black Hag. A traverse on the south-west side of the latter leads to the main ridge and the Union boundary below The Schil.

The lower slopes rise grassily in an even cone, but a rocky 'castle' breaks out of the upper northern ridge by the frontier fence. The summit lies west of the fence and takes the form of another 'castle' of bedrock and boulders. The well-worn track of the Pennine Way leads on along the frontier towards The Cheviot.

*Hen Hole*

### The Cheviot (815m)

The main mass and summit of this hill are in England, but a number of routes to it lead from the Scottish side of the border. The shortest route from Scotland starts at Sourhope at the end of one branch of the Bowmont Water valley road. A track up the Kaim Burn leads to Auchope Rig and the Stuart Lancaster Memorial Hut on the frontier ridge. A fence can be followed from here to the bouldery and conspicuous Auchope Cairn (726m) which looks across the impressive Hen Hole where rocky slopes rise to the plateau and a prominent stone man standing amidst slabs and boulders on a south-west spur of West Hill.

The Hen Hole is a very rugged pass where the College Burn turns west as it drops from a hanging valley on The Cheviot's plateau before turning north again. It is a remarkable feature in this range of rounded hills and it is well worth dropping down to it for the adventurous scramble up the path by the burn-side between the flanking buttresses.

The College valley offers an attractive but long route in from the north. A minor road from the B6351 ends at a fine row of estate buildings at Hethpool. Permits can be had outside the lambing season from J.Sale and Partners, Glendale Road, Wooler to drive to Mounthooly where a track leads into The Hen Hole.

An alternative route can be taken up a side valley to Bizzle Crags, or they can be reached from Mounthooly across West Hill where Braydon Crag is a conspicuous tor. The Bizzle Crags are the second wonder of this remarkable hill which can offer sloppy moors and near vertical crags within five minutes walking. The ascent above Bizzle Burn offers fine views to Scotland and the coast which are not seen from the summit.

The College and Bizzle burns can be useful guides in mist. Walking through the lighter vegetation by either burn is easier than taking a direct line for the summit across the spongy plateau where numerous eroded troughs bar the way.

The summit is a midden of peat, with a trig point at the centre of the morass. A fence can be used for life-support then walkers must strike out through the porridge for 20 metres on their own. The experience is messy but not dangerous if care is taken, but visits should be avoided in wet seasons.

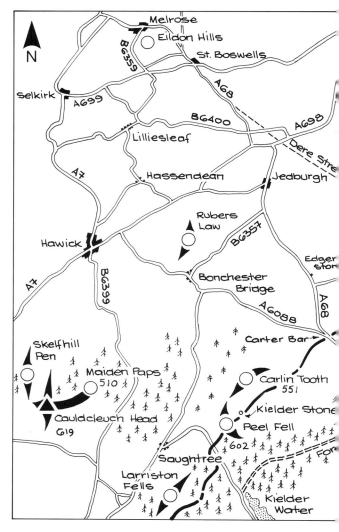

The fence near the summit leads south-west to Cairn Hill (776m) and its west top (743m) where the Union boundary fence is joined, leading on towards Windy Gyle or north-west to Auchope Cairn. The Hanging Stone is a large outcrop south-west of the 743m top. The Cheviot can also be climbed from the east from the valley of the Harthope Burn.

**Cushat Law** (615m)
This is the southernmost of four English satellite hills to The Cheviot which can be climbed from the Breamish valley. From the end of the public road at Hartside follow the road to Alnhammoor and Low Bleakhope. A broad grassy ridge leads from here to the cairn on Cushat Law.

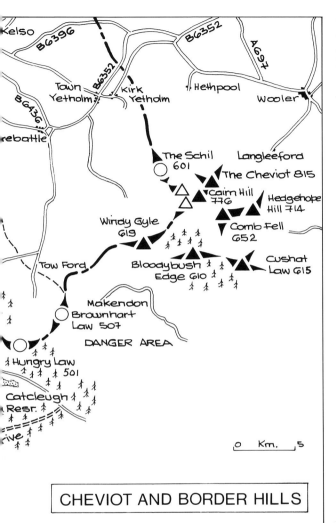

**CHEVIOT AND BORDER HILLS**

**Bloodybush Edge** (610m)
Like Cushat Law, access to this hill is from Low Bleakhope. Both hills are usually climbed together on a path by a fence between the summits which goes around the north side of Kidland Forest. The summit of Bloodybush Edge carries a trig point just south of a gate where three fences meet. One of the fences continues north towards The Cheviot along the edge of another section of forest and crosses the Salter's Road, an ancient border crossing. There are several boundary stones beyond the crossing by the fence, and two rises have to be crossed before the slopes of The Cheviot are reached at the head of the River Breamish.

**Comb Fell** (652m)
Hedgehope Hill and this hill may be ascended along with The Cheviot from the Bowmont valley on the Scottish side of the border, or the three may be reached from Langleeford on the Harthope Burn.

The ascent on a round of the Breamish valley is tedious, but can be endured for the number of summits it offers. There is no advantage in following the rough high ground all the way around the River Breamish from Bloodybush Edge. A more direct line across the upper valley towards the distinctive Coldlaw Cairn on the south ridge sacrifices height but lessens the gruelling distance.

**Hedgehope Hill** (714m)
This is the highest of the four Cheviot satellites surrounding the Breamish valley. It is easily reached from the Harthope valley to the north or from Hartside above the Breamish, where it is best left to the end of the day if a traverse of the four hills is being undertaken. The hill has a distinctive shape, with a western ridge rising into

*Looking from Windy Gyle towards The Cheviot*

a cone-shaped summit. This is crowned by a large cairn and a trig point at the meeting of three fences on a stony summit. The firmer conditions are a pleasant change from those on the neighbouring hills. The fence to the south-east is a guide on the descent to Linhope in the Breamish valley. Linhope Spout is an attractive waterfall on the route.

### Windy Gyle (619m)
This is the only hill of Donald height in the Cheviots to which Scotland can lay a half claim from its position on the frontier. It is easily reached on the Scottish side from the road-end near Kelsocleuch on the Bowmont Water. A good track goes south-west through a plantation up the narrow Kelsocleuch Rig and Windy Rig and contours under a top to join the frontier under the massive cairned summit. This cairn is thought to date from the Bronze Age, but was adopted in memory of Lord Francis Russell, a Warden of the Marches, who was murdered in a border dispute in 1585.

The fence along the frontier continues over several lesser heights towards the great bulk of The Cheviot, passing a stone man and another large cairn on the descent from Windy Gyle. A good track back to the Bowmont Water leaves the main ridge two kilometres north-east of Windy Gyle. This was an important border crossing point in the past as can be seen from the earthworks, forts and settlement sites on the descent to Cocklawfoot.

*Cocklawfoot from the site of the fort above Bowmont Water*

Following the frontier westwards from Windy Gyle, a fence zigzags over Mozie Law (552m) and Beefstand Hill (561m) to a trig point on Lamb Hill (511m) and a refuge hut (Yearning Saddle) in the col beyond. From the hut, an ancient defensive ditch can be seen running along the north edge of the frontier above a remarkably eroded valley which contains a very narrow ridge west of Lamb Hill.

A number of ancient cross-border routes pass over this central part of the Cheviot chain. The Street climbs from Coquetdale between Mozie Law and Windy Gyle and follows a switch-back route to Hownam. A Scottish variation descends to the reservoir at Heatherhope where there is a road to Hownam. From Lamb Hill a track goes past the Callaw Cairn to Greenhill to join with the last route, while another track goes in a westerly direction from Lamb Hill to Buchtrig and the Kale Water and another road to Hownam.

The absence of notable hills along this stretch of the Cheviot chain makes it unjustly neglected save for Pennine Way walkers. Numerous interesting walks can be made by linking up the footpaths.

### Brownhart Law (507m)
The Border ridge twists and turns for 25 kilometres between Windy Gyle and Carter Bar, forming no impressive summits but maintaining a fairly high altitude. Brown-

*Looking east from Buchtrig to the Cheviots*

hart Law was recognised by the Romans as a good viewpoint and there they built a signal station above Dere Street and their camps at Chew Green.

The hill can be climbed easily from Nether Hindhope on the Kale Water by a track over Whiteside Hill, or by a longer round past Upper Hindhope and Fairloans which joins the border north-east of Greyhound Law (484m). Both routes lead on down to England, the first as the Pennine Way alongside a forest and the second through the forest. The area of England south of Coquet Head and east of the forest should not be entered when red flags are flying.

**Hungry Law** (501m)
This hill can be climbed from Carter Bar, the Catcleugh Reservoir, or the Kale Water. The last approach, up the north ridge from Fairloans, allows a longer stretch of the main ridge to be tackled. The Border line is forested on its north side to the west of Hungry Law, but on its south side to the east of the summit.

# PATHS AND WALKS

A number of cross-border routes have already been mentioned as has the military zone south of the border. Walkers should be able to reach the Coquet valley from the north at all times. The area south of the Coquet is restricted when red flags are flying.

## The Pennine Way
This 400 kilometre route follows the spine of England from Derbyshire to the Scottish side of the Cheviots. On its last stage it climbs from Byrness in Redesdale to enter Scotland between Greyhound Law and Brownhart Law. Thereafter it follows the frontier past The Cheviot and drops to the Halter Burn and the end of the route at Kirk Yetholm.

## Dere Street
The Roman road from the Tyne to the Forth crosses the River Coquet to camps at Chew Green. The camps occupy a gentle slope on Brownhart Law where a signal station was in sight of Rubers Law and the Eildons. The route along the frontier is pleasantly firm as Dere Street heads for Blackhall Hill to turn Woden Law on the east and drop to Tow Ford on the Kale Water, which is still in use. The fort on Woden Law became a training area for the Romans. Dere Street continues by Pennymuir and Whitton Edge to Shotheids where a bee-line is taken for the Eildons.

CHAPTER 2

# The Western Cheviot and Border Hills

| | | |
|---|---|---|
| **Carlin Tooth** | 551m | 631 025 |
| **Peel Fell** | 602m | 626 998 |
| **Larriston Fells** | 512m | 569 921 |
| **Cauldcleuch Head** | 619m | 457 007 |
| **Maiden Paps** | 510m | 500 024 |
| **Skelfhill Pen** | 532m | 442 031 |
| **Rubers Law** | 424m | 580 156 |
| **Eildon Hills** | 422m | 548 323 |

Compared to the Eastern Cheviots, a less well-defined chain of lower hills extends westwards along the frontier beyond Carter Bar and the A68. As the altitude of the range drops towards the Solway plain there is a corresponding increase in height to the north across Liddesdale, and an extensive area of high ground forms a secondary barrier between the A7 and A68 to travellers from the south. It is in this northern area that the only Donald of the chapter is found - Cauldcleuch Head.

The A7 follows the north-south valleys of the River Esk, Ewes Water and River Teviot between Carlisle and Hawick, while the A68 joins the valley of the Jed Water from Carter Bar as it heads north to Jedburgh and the plain between the rivers Teviot and Tweed. The River Tweed forms a northern boundary to this chapter.

Carter Bar stands 418m above sea-level at the summit of the A68 as it crosses between Scotland and England. This route between the two countries was known as the Redeswire in medieval times and a Redeswire Stone, a few minutes walk north-east of the pass, commemorates an affray of 1575 which is thought to have been the last border battle. A 20 ton monolith marking the frontier by the roadside is a better known landmark but it is of modern date and was erected to put an end to the nuisance of souvenir hunters removing the border signs.

## ACCESS

The A68 from Jedburgh to Corbridge gives access to Carlin Tooth from Carter Bar. The B6357 Jedburgh-Newcastleton road passes the Larriston Fells and sends a minor road from Saughtree to Kielder under Peel Fell. A forest toll road can be driven 20 kilometres from Kielder Castle to join the A68 near Byrness in Redesdale. Cauldcleuch Head is best reached from the south by a minor road between the A7 and B6399, or it may be climbed with Skelfhill Pen from the north by a minor road heading south from Hawick between these two roads. Maiden Paps and the east side of the range can be reached from the B6399. Rubers Law is surrounded by the A698, B6358, A6088 and B6357 between Hawick and Jedburgh, which send off minor roads for easy access. The Eildon Hills are best reached from Melrose, and are surrounded by nearby roads.

## TRANSPORT

*Bus:* Edinburgh to Jedburgh, Otterburn and Newcastle; daily.
Edinburgh to Melrose, Hawick and Carlisle; daily.
Hawick to Jedburgh; daily.
Hawick to Chesters; Wednesday, Thursday and Saturday.
Hawick to Bonchester Bridge; Monday to Saturday.
Jedburgh to Chesters; schooldays and Saturday.
Hawick to Newcastleton; Monday to Saturday.
Carlisle to Newcastleton; Monday to Saturday.
Hawick to Saughtree; schooldays.
Hawick to Kielder; Wednesday (July to September).
Hexham to Kielder; Monday to Saturday

## ACCOMMODATION

Hotels at Canonbie, Langholm, Hawick, Jedburgh, Melrose, Bonchester Bridge and New-castleton.
Camp sites at Langholm, Bonchester Bridge, Jedburgh, Melrose and Hawick.
Youth Hostels at Melrose, Roberton, Byrness and Bellingham.

## MAPS

Ordnance Survey 1:50,000, Sheets 73, 79 and 80
Bartholomew 1:100,000, The Borders

The view north from Carter Bar is very fine in good visibility, but the vast spread of conifers in the near distance can depress walkers. The Wauchope Forest has virtually smothered ancient footpaths and approaches to the hills from the north.

A number of shapely little volcanic peaks occupy the northern ground of this chapter. The Eildons are probably the most easily recognised hills in the Southern Uplands, while Rubers Law, Maiden Paps, and a number of smaller hills add very distinctive shapes to their districts. None of them will overtax a fit walker and some are within the scope of geriatrics. No climber need consider them too lowly for attention. As with such illustrious peaks as Suilven and Stac Pollaidh at the other end of the country, quality does not depend on height.

## THE HILLS

**Carlin Tooth** (551m)

Carter Bar on the A68 gives a high start to this walk, which is quite strenuous due to soft conditions and is better avoided in wet seasons.

Following the fence and forest edge, the route climbs to Catcleuch Shin (544m), which is a good viewpoint for the Eastern Cheviots and the Catcleugh Reservoir. Once the ridge is gained these views are lost but a tremendous panorama continues to the north involving much of the eastern side of the Southern Uplands.

The near view along the ridge demands constant attention if walkers wish to stay dry. Myriads of white cotton-heads bob in the wind from the sedges dominating this ill-drained area. The fence leads to the trig point of Carter Fell (579m) near to a communications mast. The fence continues south-west to a top (553m) with a transition to heather underfoot, and barren grey dunes unexpectedly breaking up the landscape above a lochan. These are spoil heaps and

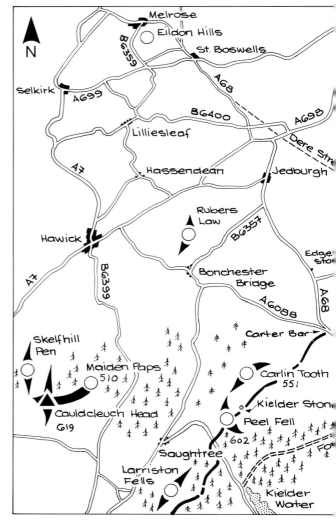

infills for drift mines when coal was worked here in the past. Numerous fragments of coal can still be picked up from the ground in what must have been a particularly wet, exposed and elevated site for this industry. Limestone was also quarried from the Meadow Cleuch to the north.

Deadwater Fell with its masts has been in front of the walker for much of this journey, but now it and the newer fence have to be ignored and a more westerly course taken over bad ground to Knox Knowe (499m) and Scrathy Holes (514m). Relics of a fence and boundary stones follow a twisting line along the higher ground until another fence is joined on the final rise. The boundary stones are about the size

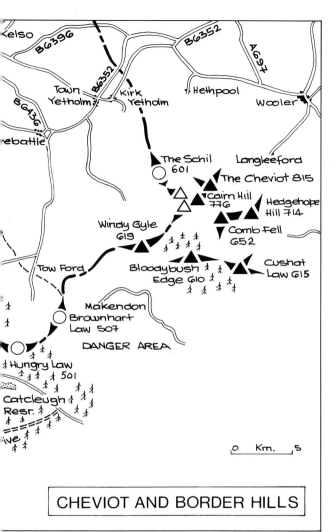

CHEVIOT AND BORDER HILLS

of traditional milestones and show an incised N for Northumberland facing England and a reversed D for Douglas facing Scotland.

Firmer ground leads to the trig point and large cairn on Carlin Tooth. The west slope of the ridge falls away dramatically with a number of rocky outcrops protruding from the scarp line. The tooth is a pointed fang about four metres high which can be climbed by an easy scramble. Short harder scrambles can be made in the vicinity. The ridge continues south-west to Hartshorn Pike (545m) where a descent leads to a col and Peel Fell.

**Peel Fell** (602m)
This is the highest of the Cheviot Hills which lie west of the A68. It is mainly a grassy and heathery hill but is scarred with eroded peat banks around the summit. A few outcrops of rock bristle from its flanks to add character. On its north-east flanks rests the Kielder Stone - one of the wonders of the Southern Uplands.

The hill can be climbed from Carlin Tooth but it is a daunting distance back to Carter Bar. A much easier route to Peel Fell starts from the Saughtree-Kielder road just south of Deadwater and about one kilometre into England. A forest road is taken up the east bank of the Deadwater Burn. Near the head of the valley this bends north-west to the Union boundary ditch and fence posts which lead to the summit. The frontier is very difficult to follow below the road. Two cairns separated by a peaty depression mark the summit of the hill. The view in clear weather is reputed to include both the east and west coasts.

To continue to the Kielder Stone follow the boundary fence north-east down a source of the Scaup Burn. The stone is a massive boulder on the north side of the burn. The fence passes above it to the west but the frontier runs through the stone.

*The Carlin Tooth (above) and the Kielder Stone (below)*

*Looking along The Catrail to Maiden Paps*

In times of strife in the past the stone was reputedly used as a letter box for communications across the border when it was too dangerous for messengers to venture into enemy territory. The boulder is composed of gritstone and gives a good scramble.

### Larriston Fells (512m)
Standing less than one kilometre inside Scotland, these south-west to north-east trending fells present a significant obstacle to cross-border travel. The turbulent history of the area is commemorated in the name Bloody Bush on the frontier where a tall tapering pillar shows toll charges for sheep, cattle, swine, and horses leading coals, and threats of prosecution for trespass to those seeking to avoid payment.

A right of way from Dinlabyre on the B6357 follows a forestry road to the south ridge of Larriston Fells where a path leads down to Bloody Bush. It is a simple expedition to combine a visit to the pillar with an ascent to the trig point at the summit of the fells. The view can include the Solway Firth and Kielder Reservoir. There is a mast on the south-west top of the fells, while to the west of the main summit three cairns at the edge of the ridge are known as The Grey Lads and once formed part of the frontier.

**Cauldcleuch Head** (619m)
This is a lone Donald in a large tract of rolling uplands between the A7 and the B6399.
A minor road along the Hermitage Water connects these roads and passes south of
the hill offering an easy approach.

From Billhope ascend to the south ridge of Stob Fell where there are good views
down the valley. Continue over Pennygant Hill and Muckle Land Knowe where a
fence leads north to Cauldcleuch Head. Three fences meet at the summit.

By continuing along the fence to the north, the Langtae Sike can be turned and a
return journey made over Langtae Hill (544m), Millstone Edge (565m) and Tudhope
Hill (699m) with a fence for help in mist.

The return from the trig point on Tudhope Hill follows the west side of a forest
to the road, or a firebreak can be taken east from the west corner of the forest to join
a road heading south.

**Maiden Paps** (510m)
From a high point of the A7 between Selkirk and Hawick the panorama of peaks to
the south is one of the most distinctive landscapes in the Southern Uplands. The
rolling border hills are enlivened here as nowhere else by jutting volcanic peaks.
Maiden Paps are an eye-catching pair in this scene.

The B6399 south of Hawick passes east of the pair but a forest lies in the way. A
farm road to Sundhope can be walked through the southern edge of the trees and a
route taken up Sundhope Rig to the edge of the forest at Black Rig. Leap Hill rises
dramatically above the forest to the east while the higher Greatmoor Hill shows less
interesting bulk to the west.

The route to Maiden Paps lies over Scaw'd Law where the narrow ridge has been
left unplanted. It is hard going over cushions of heather, cloudberry and moss, but
this gives way to grasses and clumps of lady's bedstraw on the summits, with a
bouldery cleft between. The aptness of the name bestowed on the two cones is best
appreciated from Scaw'd Law, with a similar pair of Eildons lying beyond. The hills
also look to Rubers Law beyond the viaduct at Shankend on the former Waverley
rail route from Edinburgh to Carlisle. The route had its summit at the Whitrope
Tunnel east of Leap Hill and sections of the route offer good walking.

A mysterious ditch known as The Catrail crosses the forest north of Maiden Paps.
This may date from the Iron Age or earlier and has been left unplanted. It can be
reached by a firebreak from Maiden Paps and offers an interesting but very rough
route back to the B6399.

**Skelfhill Pen** (532m)
This rocky and shapely little peak forms an attractive introduction to the higher ground when coming south of Hawick between the River Teviot and the Slitrig Water. It is easily climbed from the minor road which runs south-south-west from Hawick past the Motte to the Allan Water and Skelfhill Burn.

A car can be left west of Priesthaugh by the Skelfhill Burn and the side road taken past Skelfhill. The north-east ridge is pleasantly grassy and leads over a small top to the impressively steep summit cone. The drum-shaped cairn by the trig point is a good landmark from the surrounding hills. A route round the valley can be made over White Hill (473m), Millstone Edge (565m), and Langtae Hill (544m) to Cauld-cleuch Head and a return made over Skelfhill Fell (533m) and along the Holywell Rig to Priesthaugh.

**Rubers Law** (424m)
The volcanic cone of Rubers Law is a well-known landmark in the Borders despite its modest height. The hill may have been used by the Romans as a signal station as it sits on its own with wide views and incorporates dressed stone in its walls suggestive of Roman work. Public roads come close on all sides so access is simple. One route starts from north of Hallrule two and a half kilometres north of Bonchester Bridge and follows a farm track straight across the contours until a plantation is rounded on its south side to gain the south ridge. A continuous dyke meanders around the hill with a number of gates leading through.

A heathery south top lies about half a kilometre from the main summit which has been dramatically shaped by nature and early man into a steep little fortress. Cliffs to the west of the trig point fall about six metres to a boulder field within the ditch of the ancient stronghold.

**The Eildon Hills** (404m, 422m, and 371m)
The Eildons rise picturesquely to the south of the River Tweed at Melrose. The triple peaks are the remnants of a composite laccolith, formed by lava welling up into domes below sedimentary rocks which have since been eroded away. The Mid Hill is the highest peak and sits between Eildon North and Eildon Wester - though the last might have been more usefully called Eildon South! At a later stage volcanic activity recurred to form the Little Hill which now stands as a hard plug of basalt above Bowdenmoor Reservoir.

The legend of King Arthur and his knights asleep within a hill awaiting the call to action is linked with the Little Hill, while Michael Scott the Wizard, Thomas the Rhymer and Sir Walter Scott are also associated with the Eildons.

*Rubers Law from the south-east*

The hills can be climbed from Melrose leaving the B6359 just out of the town by a signposted path. The track heads for the col between the Mid and North hills while a branch heads round the north side of Eildon North to Newstead. The track from Newstead sends a branch round the south side of Eildon North and the Mid Hill.

Because of their detached and far-seen and far-seeing situation, the Eildons have been important hills through history. An Iron Age fort on Eildon North has yielded evidence of some 300 hut circles. These are represented today by mounds scattered over the slopes between the summit and the outer ditches of this former hill town. A natural shelf within the fort on the south-east shows ridge and furrow cultivation.

The Romans took over Eildon North from the settlements of the Selgovae tribe and erected a signal station on the hill above their great camp at Trimontium *(the place of the three hills)* which lay below at Newstead and is commemorated by a monument erected in 1927.

The Mid Hill is the major summit of the range and had a view indicator erected on it by public subscription to the memory of Sir Walter Scott, who was "wont to view and point the glories of the Borderland" from this spot.

*Middle Eildon from Bowdenmoor*

The Ministry of Defence has extended its control into the Eildons recently. Red and white poles and warning notices now surround the Mid Hill to keep walkers off when firing is taking place at the range at the foot of the west face. The situation is very unsatisfactory for those who would come a distance to climb the Eildons, but it has apparently developed with a minimum of protest. The Eildon Hills and Leaderfoot was designated as one of Scotland's National Scenic Areas by the Countryside Commission for Scotland. It deserves better than to be treated as a military range.

# CHAPTER 3

# The Lammermuir Hills

| | | |
|---|---|---|
| **Meikle Says Law** | 535m | 581 617 |
| **Lammer Law** | 527m | 524 618 |
| **Twin Law** | 447m | 625 548 |
| **Dirrington Great Law** | 398m | 698 549 |
| **Dirrington Little Law** | 363m | 687 531 |
| **Traprain Law** | 221m | 581 747 |

The Lammermuirs are the most north-easterly group of hills in the Southern Uplands. They run from The A7 Edinburgh to Galashiels road east to the North Sea and are bounded to the south by the Merse of Berwickshire and the River Tweed, and to the north by the Firth of Forth and the Lothian plain.

Not even the most ardent enthusiast for this range could claim that its hills are exciting. The area is more of an elevated moorland plateau rather than a range of hills and is ideally suited to climbers nervous of steep ground! The range has its own special attractions though for those who are genuinely interested in landscape and the structure of the countryside, and it awards numerous surprises to those who explore its hidden recesses.

The most obvious feature of the range is its clearly defined northern edge which runs in a south-west to north-east direction separating the Central Lowlands to the north from the Southern Uplands. This is the often quoted Dunbar to Girvan fault-line where the land to the north has subsided and the older rocks to the south have been uplifted.

The shortage of distinctive hills in the Lammermuirs can lead to problems for careless map-readers, in good visibility as well as mist. With few points of distinction, more care than usual needs to be taken in navigation if the shortest route is to be followed. The relatively low summits and generally drier air of the east side of the country makes hill-fog less of a problem than in the west.

The Lammermuirs are a formidable barrier to travellers. Snow gates on the A68 between Pathhead and Oxton check the foolhardy at times of blizzards, while those driving south-east from Gifford and Garvald face fierce gradients in leaving the lowlands.

### ACCESS

The A1 from north-east England or the Edinburgh area. The B6355 leaving the A1 at Tranent is a fairly direct route into the heart of the range. This road is joined near Gifford by the B6370 running from Dunbar along the northern edge of the range. The B6355 cuts the range in two with the higher hills on the south side. Near its highest point, the B6355 sends off a branch south-east to Duns from which a number of lesser routes head west up the Dye Water and Watch Water. The B6355 also sends a branch north-westwards to Garvald up the Whiteadder Water. South of Gifford, minor roads lead up the Hopes Water to West Hopes. The B6456 on the southern edge of the range can be useful for reaching Dirrington Great Law, Dirrington Little Law, and Twin Law, or as starting points for cross-country routes. The A7 and A68 are roughly parallel routes marking the western boundary of this chapter. The B6368 runs between them, and at Soutra Hill joins with the Roman road from England to the Lothians. East of the A68 and A697 a number of routes lead into the hills but parking places are scarce on access roads except for the public road running to Tollishill.

### TRANSPORT

*Bus:* Edinburgh to Haddington, Innerwick and Berwick; daily.
Edinburgh to Oxton and Jedburgh or Kelso; daily.
Edinburgh to Pencaitland; daily.
Haddington to Gifford and Humbie; Monday and Wednesday.
Haddington to Longyester and Garvald; Tuesday.
Haddington to Garvald, Stenton and Dunbar; Saturday.
Galashiels to Duns and Berwick; daily.
Galashiels to Westruther, Duns and Eyemouth; Tuesday and Thursday.

*Postbus:* Duns to Longformacus; schooldays and Tuesday, Thursday and Saturday.

### ACCOMMODATION

Hotels at Pathhead, Haddington, East Linton, Garvald, Gifford, Humbie, Greenlaw, Lauder, Longformacus, Oxton, Cockburnspath and Duns. Camping at Haddington, Greenlaw, Cockburnspath, Lauder and Longformacus.
Youth hostels at Abbey St Bathans and Coldingham.

### MAPS

Ordnance Survey 1:50,000, Sheets 66 and 67
Bartholomew 1:100,000, Edinburgh and the Forth

Even on the coastal fringe of the range to the east, the A1 and Edinburgh to London railway line have to wriggle their ways over a watershed at Grantshouse to pass the region. The collapse of a tunnel on the railway at Penmanshiel in 1979 led to massive excavations to create a new valley for the route. Where the railway chooses to follow the top of the sea-cliffs, erosion is a constant problem.

The coastal scenery on the eastern edge of the Lammermuirs is splendid and the entire coast-line from Berwick to North Berwick is worth exploring. St Abbs's Head has the highest sea-cliffs on the mainland of Southern Scotland, rising over 100m. A coastal walk goes south from St Abb's Head to St Abbs and Eyemouth, and a route can be made in the opposite direction to the spectacularly sited Fast Castle, though fences have to be crossed. Reference has already been made in the introduction to

*Hopes Reservoir and Lammer Law from Hope Hills*

the important geological site at Siccar Point west of Fast Castle. The John Muir Country park at Dunbar offers some fine coastal walking„ while there are secluded harbours at Cove and Burnmouth in impressive settings.

## THE HILLS

**Meikle Says Law** (535m)
The Lammermuirs rise to their highest elevation on this hill - though hill is not altogether an appropriate term in such rolling, undramatic scenery. The location is easily reached from the Gifford to Longformacus road at the Redstone Rig. A car can be left at the road ends to Faseny Cottage and Mayshiel provided access is left clear to east and west.

The walk starts downhill to Faseny Cottage, where roads branch left and right along the Faseny Burn and straight ahead up the Lamb Burn. This last route heads straight for Meikle Says Law branching right for Dun Side where a left branch descends to cross the burn. A well graded vehicular track curves up Dun Side and leads to the trig point on the summit of Meikle Says Law where a fence runs up from the south-east. This fence continues south-west towards the undistinguished Willie's Law (496m), but a more interesting route returns north-east along the Lammermuir Edge.

*Traprain Law from the south*

A road starts by the fence on the south-west side of Meikle Says Law and curves downhill by the sources of the Faseny Water, following the valley back to Faseny Cottage. The road can be used for about one kilometre and an ascent made to the Whitestone Cairn on Harestone Hill. The walk along the northern edge of the range back to the B6355 can give good views over the Central Lowlands to the Highlands, while Dirrington Great Law, The Cheviot, Twin Law and the Eildons can show up well to the south.

### Lammer Law (527m)
This hill stands at the north-west edge of the range and is cut off from the main plateau by the deep trench of the Hopes Water. For that reason, it is a more shapely hill than points farther east and is also a much better viewpoint.

The quickest route to the hill is to follow the vehicle track from Longyester, south of Gifford, which can be driven to just past Blinkbonny Wood. This track passes about half a kilometre east of Lammer Law and is a very easy route to the hill.

A more interesting route starts from West Hopes and goes up a north ridge of Hope Hills. Tracks cross an aqueduct and climb through heather for fine views of Lammer Law over the Hopes Reservoir. The plateau comes as an anti-climax and shuts out the views. Lowrans Law (497m) and Seenes Law (513m) beyond a fence are mere undulations on the moor rising to Meikle Says Law. Lammer Law is

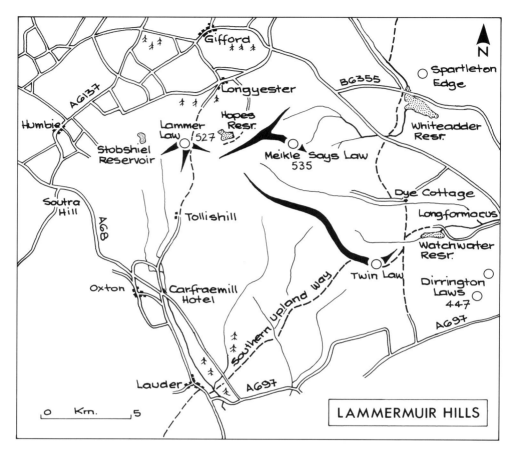

LAMMERMUIR HILLS

reached over Bullhope Law, joining the Longyester-Tollishill track under the north top of Crib Law. A branch in this track to the west leads to Crib Law (509m) where there is a gate in a fence.

To reach Lammer Law follow the Longyester track north to the col and take a left branch which swings round to the summit from the north. From the large cairn and trig point the Pentlands are prominent.

A return to West Hopes can be made down the east ridge to Bleak Law which is another fine viewpoint for the reservoir. A road along the south side of the reservoir leads out to West Hopes through an area of juniper and deciduous woodlands.

### Twin Law (447m)

The road west from Longformacus to the Watch Water Reservoir brings this most distinctive of Lammermuir summits within easy reach. Cars can be driven across the dam to a parking area beside the track leading to Scarlaw. The route goes west past Scarlaw and looks to the Dirrington Laws over the reservoir. At a crossing of vehicle tracks the south track is taken to a ford and footbridge over the Watch Water where there is a well and memorial to a keeper from Rawburn. Continue south on the track until past a small plantation, then ascend the east-north-east ridge by a fence to Twin Law. This entire route is on the line of the Southern Upland Way.

The summit is remarkable for its two great cairns which are recognisable from a long distance. The two stone heaps stand about 100 metres apart and each supports a small broch-shaped tower. Both structures have a recessed seat facing south while the more westerly cairn has a trench through the stones leading to a stepped approach to the tower.

Tradition links the cairns with two brothers who mortally wounded each other as champions of two armies - each unaware of the other's identity as they had been separated in childhood.

### Dirrington Great Law (398m)
### Dirrington Little Law (363m)

These shapely little hills of small stature can be climbed together from The B6456 Duns-Westruther road. A path leads north from a high point of the road to the Little Law. A direct line to the north-east past Kippetlaw leads on to the Great Law, and a return can be made to the B6456 by using the track south from the Hallywell Rig.

Both hills are heathery and have degraded burial mounds on their summits. The Great Law has two - one on either side of a trig point. There are unusual field formations north-west of the Great Law towards Dronshiel - which is a short way to this hill from the Longformacus to Duns road.

The Little Law is a good vantage point for the Kaims which lie to the south side of the B6456. These form a remarkable twisting line of glacial debris which was deposited under an ice sheet moving across the area. This is one of the best examples of an esker to be seen in Scotland and is well worth a walk to the south for a closer look.

### Traprain Law (221m)

This is a conspicuous little hill south-west of East Linton. It was formed by an igneous intrusion solidifying in a dome under other rocks which have now been eroded away. The hill can be climbed easily from the road on the north side. The east side has suffered greatly from quarrying.

An Iron Age fort on the hill yielded a large treasure in 1919 which can be seen in the Museum of Antiquities in Edinburgh. A large rock near the summit is separated from a smaller boulder by a narrow passage and is known as the Maiden Stone. A monolith called the Loth Stone can be found near the south-west end of the hill on the west side of the road, while another standing stone sits half a kilometre farther south. Two more north of the A1 on either side of East Linton suggest a connection with Traprain Law.

The hill has a steep rocky south face which offers good rock climbing.

## PATHS AND WALKS

*Longyester to Tollishill.* This route crosses the eastern slopes of Lammer Law and Crib Law and descends to Tollishill past a small standing stone. A public road at Tollishill leads to the A697. (7 kilometres between gates).

*Dere Street.* A section of the Roman road between the Eildons and the Lothians has been identified between Oxton and Soutra Hill. Follow the minor road north-west from Oxton to the church at Channelkirk (482 545) and continue towards Kirktonhill. At a fork in the road go round the north side of the farm to a cottage and join the track running northwards on the west side of the remains of a Roman camp. A forestry plantation west of Turf Law has obscured the old road, so go along the east side of the forest to King's Inch where a gap in the trees leads to the B6368 near the medieval hospice of Soutra Aisle. Views to the south on this walk look to the mega-milestones of Black Hill and the Eildons en route to the Cheviots and Rome. (8 kilometres).

*Dunbar to Wedderlie.* A number of routes starting from Dunbar are associated with the herring trade which provided inland communities with an important part of their diet. The first eight kilometres or so from Dunbar follow public vehicular roads today. Walking has to start near Hartside (654 723) where the Herring Road turns east then south to climb over Lothian Edge with remarkable near views of glacial melt-water channels. The first of numerous branch routes crosses Watch Law at a gate towards Cranshaws while the major route heads south-west to another gate to cross the Mossy Burn. The south-east edge of a forest is joined on Dunbar Common to cross the West Burn and continue by a firebreak to a forest road. The road joins power lines heading south-west and meets the public road where the Kingside Burn meets the Whiteadder Water. The route can be followed on past the west end of Whiteadder Reservoir to Dye Cottage on the Dye Water and across the Watch Water to Wedderlie and the B6456 east of Westruther. (34 kilometres).

*Pencaitland railway walk.* The former railway route can be followed from West Saltoun past Pencaitland and Ormiston to the A6124 at Crossgatehall. (12 kilometres).

*Haddington to Longniddry railway walk.* A walk from Haddington along the former railway track ends at Longniddry where the main-line station is still open. (7 kilometres).

# CHAPTER 4

# The Moorfoot Hills

| | | |
|---|---|---|
| **Dundreich** | 623m | 275 491 |
| **Bowbeat Hill** | 626m | 292 469 |
| **Blackhope Scar** | 651m | 315 484 |
| **Whitehope Law** | 623m | 331 446 |
| **Windlestraw Law** | 659m | 372 431 |
| **Dunslair Heights** | 602m | 287 437 |
| **Lee Pen** | 502m | 326 386 |

## ACCESS
The A72 along the Tweed valley and B6372 Penicuik to Gorebridge road along the northern edge of the range are the main approaches from east and west. The A703 Leadburn to Peebles and B7007 and B709 Middleton to Innerleithen roads give access from north and south. Minor roads to Gladhouse Reservoir and Portmore Loch are useful in the north-west. The A701 in the west and A7 in the east are outer boundaries among the foothills.

## TRANSPORT
*Bus:* Edinburgh to Eddleston, Peebles and Galashiels; daily.
Edinburgh to Stow and Galashiels; daily.
Peebles to Romannobridge and West Linton; daily.

## ACCOMMODATION
Hotels at Arniston, Gorebridge, Pathhead, Leadburn, Middleton, Clovenfords, Galashiels, Innerleithen, Peebles, Stow and Walkerburn.
Camping at Dalkeith, Galashiels, Innerleithen, Peebles and Melrose.
Youth Hostels at Melrose and Edinburgh.

## MAPS
Ordnance Survey 1:50,000, Sheet 73
Bartholomew 1:100,000, The Borders

The Moorfoots lie between the Lothian plain and the Tweed Valley and are sandwiched between the Pentlands and the Lammermuirs. With the Lammermuirs they form a distinctive northern edge to the Southern Uplands, maintaining a very regular north-east to south-west line which separates the hill-country from the Central Lowlands of the Forth basin.

As in the Lammermuirs, the highest summits are less a range of hills and more an elevated plateau with few distinguishing features. The plateau-like character tends to cause water-logging on the broader ridges where rainfall does not escape readily to the valleys, and walking conditions can be more arduous than might be expected.

With the exception of the isolated Windlestraw Law, the higher hills of the range are grouped in a horseshoe-shaped ridge running round the upper valley of the River South Esk. This river drains northwards into the wide but shallow Gladhouse Reservoir, which is a conspicuous feature of the landscape and an important wintering area for large numbers of geese.

A glacial breach between the valleys of the Glentress Water and the Dewar Burn, now used by the B709, separates this northern and western group of hills from Windlestraw Law to the east – the only Donald in a large tract of fairly open country stretching to the Gala Water.

The northern and eastern parts of the range are given over mainly to farming and shooting while much of the southern and western section is under forest. Glentress Forest between Peebles and Innerleithen is the oldest forest in the south of Scotland planted by the Forestry Commission. Parts of this land are now producing their second crop of trees while the extensive network of forest roads is open to walkers, cyclists, pony trekkers and wayfarers.

The large forests along the valley of the River Tweed have altered the landscape considerably, but views from some of the smaller hills north of the river are among the finest in the Southern Uplands. Whether the forests have impaired or enhanced the views depends on people's attitudes to trees. Views are more restricted now and have to be worked up to through the forests, but many vistas are still extensive and are well worth seeking out.

## THE HILLS

### Dundreich (623m)
Also known as Jeffries Corse, this is the most northerly and westerly of the higher hills in the Moorfoots. It sits on the west side of the River South Esk's valley and can be reached with little effort from Moorfoot at the south end of Gladhouse Reservoir.

The track from Moorfoot can be followed south up the South Esk's valley until Gladhouse Cottage is passed. Stay on the west bank but cross the burns coming down from Jeffries Corse and ascend a well-defined ridge. The path to the west takes a slightly more direct line but uses a duller slope. Both routes join up as grass gives way to heather on the upper slopes of a north top (611m). A fence leads on 800 metres to the cairn and trig point on Dundreich, the summit named Jeffries Corse in Donald's Tables.

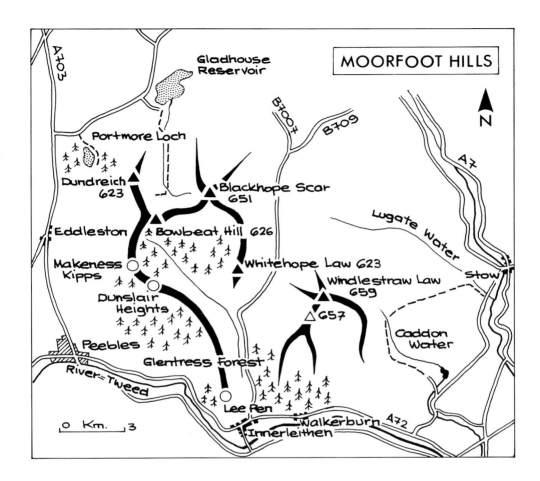

Another easy approach to the hill starts from Westloch in the north-west and follows the road to Portmore Loch. Go round the loch and ascend near the north edge of the plantation to Loch Hill and a good ridge to the summit. To the south of Dundreich a west ridge can be taken back to Portmore Loch, or a south ridge can be walked over Hog Knowes to Cardon Law and Dunslair Heights along the edges of the forest. This route avoids the Donalds which lie along a ridge going south-east from Dundreich.

### Bowbeat Hill (626m)

On its own, this hill could be climbed in a straightforward ascent from the track which runs up the South Esk valley from Gladhouse Reservoir. Walkers are more likely to reach it in a round of the valley from Dundreich or Blackhope Scar.

The approach from Dundreich requires an eastward course over a slight rise followed by a south-east course to turn the upper reaches of the Leithen Water. The broad ridge is cloaked in coarse vegetation and turns south eventually to join a fence

*Hirendean Castle and The Kipps*

rising over a 582m height above the forested slopes to the west. The fence continues south-east to a col then bends eastwards over Bowbeat Hill.

There is an interesting view along the V-shaped trough of the South Esk valley to Gladhouse Reservoir and Edinburgh from the summit. A north-east ridge leads on with the fence over Emly Bank (604m) and drops to a col under Blackhope Scar.

### Blackhope Scar (651m)

This hill is most easily climbed from Moorfoot at the south end of the Gladhouse Reservoir. The track is followed to Gladhouse Cottage where a bridge over the River South Esk allows access to the ruined tower house of Hirendean above a group of hardy trees. The castle stands on a ridge which gives a good view back to the reservoir and is a quick way onto the higher ground at The Kipps (541m). This top can also be reached by a track going up the corrie south of The Kipps from the South Esk. The plateau is hard going once grass gives way to heather.

Another route from the valley uses the rough road by the South Esk until opposite Blackhope Scar, then climbs by Long Cleave to the summit past the source of the river. If approaching from Bowbeat Hill, a fence can be followed up the south-west ridge. This joins onto a fence from the south ridge and runs over the summit and down the north-west ridge.

*Gladhouse Reservoir*

The B709 at its summit north of Innerleithen offers a temptingly high starting point for the hill where a V-shaped cleft separates the western Moorfoots from Windlestraw Law. The Piper's Grave at the summit of the road marks the spot where, according to tradition, a piper expired while attempting to play his pipes all the way from Peebles to Lauder.

The closely packed contours of the valley contrast greatly with those on the plateau leading to Blackhope Scar and should warn astute walkers of the damp and tedious going in front of them. One has to admire the tenacity of those who succeeded in laying a fence across Garvald Punks which shows the way along the high ground. Numerous eroded trenches gape on Rough Moss and make an approach from the north-east even more arduous.

### Whitehope Law (623m)
The B709 offers an easy approach to this hill from about two kilometres south of the summit of the road. The ascent can be combined with that of Blackhope Scar across the tiring intervening ground, but it takes special dedication to do the round of the South Esk Donalds from Gladhouse and go all the way out to Whitehope Law and have to face the journey back.

**Windlestraw Law** (659m)
This is the highest hill in the Moorfoots. It is separated from the other Donalds by the B709 Innerleithen to Heriot road. The hill can be climbed quickly from the summit of this road, but the going is heavy underfoot and the view dull.

A much finer route starts from Walkerburn where the A72 crosses the Walker Burn beside a listed building of architectural merit – the 19th century cast iron urinal! By crossing the fence at the side of the bridge the east bank of the burn can be followed north, but it is more courteous to ask permission at the farm on the west bank and walk through the yard.

A road up the west bank leads through the forest to the ruined house at Priesthope. As the steep V-shaped valley twists about, the outside world is quickly left behind and the finer character of these hills is appreciated more than their high moorlands wastes.

Continue northwards by the burn until it splits and take a path up the ridge between the two waters. After a slight drop a fence is met coming in from the west, and this is followed north-east to the south-west top of Windlestraw Law (657m) where there is a cairn. A dip of 30m leads onto the north-east ridge, running one and a half kilometres with the fence to the main summit where a trig point sits at the junction of three fences.

A good route back leaves the south-west top and follows the ridge south-south-east to Scawd Law. A vehicle track runs along this ridge and lightens the trudge through the heather. Carry on south to Cairn Hill, which is surrounded by forest to west, south and east. This can give a very good view of the Tweed valley, the Minchmoor, Innerleithen and the Tweedsmuir Hills. A firebreak leads south from the summit towards Walkerburn and passes the remains of a second chambered cairn about 120m below the summit cairn. At the foot of the forest a high wall has to be turned to the right to regain the road.

Windlestraw Law can also be climbed from Innerleithen. Cars can be left on the west side of the Leithen Water near the start of the B709. Cross the Cuddy Bridge of 1701 (333 371) and follow a path up through the woods on the crest of the ridge. An ancient fort is passed above the trees, showing three ditches on the steep drop to the col beyond before the ridge rises again to Pirn Craig. The view back is one of the best in the Borders, with Innerleithen curving above and around the fort in a fish-eye panorama which includes the Tweed valley, the Minchmoor and the Tweedsmuir Hills.

A firebreak continues up the crest of the ridge to Kirnie Law. In the col between Kirnie Law and Priesthope Hill there is an astonishing ruined enclosure of reinforced concrete which is the size of a football stadium with walls five metres high. Were it surrounded by desert instead of heather it could be mistaken for a Foreign Legion fort, but it was built around 1921 as a reservoir for the mills at Walkerburn. The mounded course of a pipe-line running up to a tower to the south-east of Kirnie Law is evidence of a pioneering pumped storage scheme which operated until the Second

*The River Tweed below Peebles*

World War, lifting water 300m from the Tweed at night to power the mills during the day. A large hole was blasted in the wall of the reservoir in 1990. From Priesthope Hill the ridge continues north to Glede Knowe and joins the south-west ridge of Windlestraw Law.

Another interesting route to the hill starts at a forest car-park at Thornylee about five kilometres east of Walkerburn. Follow the longest of the waymarked forest trails to its summit above the forest on Thornylee Craigs where there is another splendid viewpoint. A long ridge continues over Southerly Nick and Stony Knowe to Seathope Law (542m) where three fences meet east of the summit. The heathery route continues past Maiden Law and Redscar Law to the grassy Windlestraw Law.

**Dunslair Heights** (602m)
Although not high enough to be a Donald, this hill is the crown of a considerable area of interesting country in the south of the Moorfoots. It stands four and a half kilometres north-east of Peebles and is mostly surrounded by forest, but may be reached by several routes. An expedition from the east combines forest and ridge scenery.

*Innerleithen from Pirn Craig*

The route starts from the B709 about six kilometres north of Innerleithen and follows the north bank of the Leithen Water through the Rosebery estate on a right of way which leads to Peebles. The road is followed past Leithen Lodge and Williamslee, until the steep V-shaped valley is left on the south side of the ruined Craighope and a road is climbed up a prominent ridge in the direction of Makeness Kipps. Where the road ends, take the right-hand branch of the burn to join a road. This leads south-east heading for Williamslee, but leave it at a firebreak on the west which gives access to the broad heathery clearance running between Makeness Kipps and Dunslair Heights. The summit of the latter has accumulated various buildings and environmental research equipment.

The hill can be climbed from Glentress Forest on the south where information boards aid navigation. Those returning to the B709 should follow a firebreak leading south-east onto the road to Williamslee, or the unplanted side of the ridge wall can be followed over Black Law and Black Knowe to Lee Pen.

Dunslair Heights can also be climbed from Peebles by following the road up the east bank of the Soonhope Burn. Walk past the front of the Outdoor Centre at Shieldgreen and take the path starting behind it into the forest. This passes the remains of Shieldgreen Tower and crosses two roads as it climbs to the col between Dunslair Heights and Makeness Kipps.

**Lee Pen** (502m)

The peaked summit of this hill is prominent in the junction between the Leithen Water and the River Tweed. It can be climbed easily from Innerleithen, gaining the ridge between an ancient fort and St Ronan's Wells. Both are worth a visit.

The summit makes a fine climax to the ridge-walk from Dunslair Heights as it is another very fine viewpoint for the Borders. A descent from it to the north-east leads to a gap in a wood and a track to the B709 where it crosses the Leithen Water at the golf course.

## PATHS AND WALKS

*Stow to Blackhaugh.* The Gala Water is crossed at Stow and the road taken south on the west bank. A side road leads through the farmyard at Lugate and the right branch taken past the Lodge. Continue up the Back Burn and slant uphill to pass through a gap in the inside corner of an L-shaped shelter belt. A vehicle track leads onto the north shoulder of Dunlee Hill, where a fence can be followed north to the col to descend the burn to the lonely house of Scroof in a grove of ash and rowan. The track out from there follows the Caddon Water past Caddonhead then climbs over a col to cross the Caddon Water at Blackhaugh and rejoin the minor road from Stow heading for the B710 to Clovenfords. (17 kilometres).

*West Linton to Peebles.* This route is the continuation of the old drove road over the Cauldstane Slap in the Pentlands. Its start is obscured by the expansion of West Linton and roads to the south so the walking need not start until near Romanno-bridge. From the cemetery one kilometre north-east of Romannobridge, the route goes south-east from the A701, passing north of Romanno House and following a track uphill to cross a col north of Drum Maw and descend to cross the Fingland Burn. The track goes round the south end of Green Knowe and enters a forest by a gate north of the Flemington Burn. The route climbs to join a road which bypasses Greenside. Just past Greenside a firebreak is taken east straight up the hill. This crosses a ride going along the ridge and drops to Upper Stewarton (217 460). Go east at Stewarton Toll (220 455), join the road from Eddleston towards the Meldon Hills and take the east branch to Upper Kidston. Go east through the fields along the south side of a shelter belt and climb round the north side of Hamilton Hill to descend to Rosetta and Peebles. The descent between dykes is on a track worn down to the bedrock, reflecting heavy use on this historic approach to the bridge over the Tweed. (20 kilometres).

*Penicuik to Bonnyrigg.* A route along an old railway track following the north bank of the North Esk River from the A701. Highlights include Sir Thomas Bouch's Firth Viaduct and two tunnels. (10 kilometres).

# CHAPTER 5

# Arthur's Seat and the Pentland Hills

| | | |
|---|---|---|
| **Arthur's Seat** | 251m | 275 730 |
| **Caerketton Hill** | 478m | 237 662 |
| **Allermuir Hill** | 493m | 227 662 |
| **Castlelaw Hill** | 488m | 225 648 |
| **Turnhouse Hill** | 506m | 213 627 |
| **Carnethy Hill** | 573m | 204 619 |
| **Scald Law** | 579m | 192 611 |
| **West Kip** | 551m | 178 606 |
| **Black Hill** | 501m | 188 632 |
| **East Cairn Hill** | 567m | 129 593 |
| **West Cairn Hill** | 562m | 107 584 |

Although the Pentlands lie within the zone of the Central Lowlands, they form one of the most distinctive hill ranges in the southern half of Scotland. Arthur's Seat stands farther to the north and is lower, but must also be included in this guide as it is such a splendid little peak and is probably the most climbed hill in Scotland. Together, Arthur's Seat and the Pentlands form a dynamic backcloth to the city of Edinburgh and deserve much of the credit for that city's international reputation. Edinburgh without its hills would be a less exciting scene.

The Pentlands lie on the northern side of the Southern Uplands boundary fault, but they follow the same north-east to south-west trend as hill ranges south of the fault. The valleys of the Water of Leith and the River North Esk also follow this trend as they bound the Pentlands on the north-west and south-east.

There are no Donalds in this range, but those who ignore these hills on that account make a great mistake. There is a pleasing vitality of shape about the volcanic hills of the northern half of the range. A number of the summits take peaked form and can even be mistaken for Highland Munros when seen from various parts of the Southern Uplands. The south-western end of the range tails away into moorland and lower hills around Dunsyre and is much less often visited.

### ACCESS
Arthur's Seat dominates Holyrood Park at the foot of Edinburgh's High Street and is surrounded by access roads. The Pentlands are neatly contained within the A720 Edinburgh by-pass and A721 Carnwath to Melbourne roads to the north and south, and the A70 Edinburgh to Carnwath and A702 Edinburgh to Biggar roads to the north-west and south-east. Minor roads intrude from these into the range, notably at Dunsyre, Garvald, West Linton, Balerno and Currie. The access road to Loganlea and Glencorse reservoirs is open to walkers but not cars which must be left at the Flotterstone Visitor Centre near the start of the road.

### TRANSPORT
*Bus:* Edinburgh to Biggar; daily.
Edinburgh to Balerno; daily.
Edinburgh local services to Hillend, Oxgangs and Colinton; daily.
Carnwath to Biggar; Tuesday, Thursday and Saturday.
Balerno to Carnwath; Sunday.

*Train:* It is easy to disembark at Edinburgh's two mainline stations and enjoy a variety of outings in this range in conjunction with buses, while local stations at Wester Hailes and Curriehill are not far from the hills.

### ACCOMMODATION
Hotels at Loanhead, Penicuik, Roslin, Nine Mile Burn, Bonnyrigg, Lasswade, Livingston, Carnwath, Dolphinton and West Linton.

Camping at Dalkeith.
Youth Hostels at Edinburgh.

### MAPS
Ordnance Survey 1:50,000, Sheets 65, 66 and 72.
Bartholomew 1:42,240, Pentland Hills.

The summits of the Pentlands are arranged in a northern group standing north of Glencorse Reservoir, a continuous chain separating the glen of the Logan Burn from the A702, a line of hills north of the Logan Burn, and a western group arranged around the sources of the Lyne Water..

With a capital city and a number of towns grouped around the range, the Pentlands come under considerable pressure from people engaged in a wide variety of pursuits. The major summits are all included in the Pentland Hills Regional Park, while Bonaly Country Park and Hillend Country Park are smaller designated areas within the regional park which are designed to control pressure points where city-dwellers spill into the country in greatest numbers.

The Regional Park has a visitor centre at Flotterstone on the Glencorse Burn just west of the A702. Hillend has a very popular dry-ski slope and visitor facilities while Bonaly has toilets and car parks but is less developed. Regional Park Authority thinking conflicts with the right to roam. Walkers unwilling to conform to regula-

*Glencorse Reservoir and Turnhouse Hill*

tions regarding access should act discreetly, should not break rules without cause, and should consider the effect of their actions on future visitors. At the same time, walkers need to be vigilant in defending their rights, as were those who bequeathed to us so many footpaths and rights of way in the area. The Ministry of Defence, to instance one user, is inclined to act arbitrarily in its own interests, and has interfered with rights of way in the past. The MOD has a live-firing range on the south side of Castlelaw Hill which is frequently in use, during which times the public are excluded for their safety. Walkers, rightly, have to leave their vehicles outside the Logan Glen. Some walkers might feel more sympathetic to the park concept if mountain bikes and the vehicles of soldiers, fishers and others were less of a hazard on the narrow road.

A number of reservoirs in the range provide water for the Edinburgh area. Glencorse and Loganlea reservoirs are particularly important features in the landscape amidst the higher hills.

## THE HILLS

### Arthur's Seat (251m)

Edinburgh's citizens are fortunate to have this marvellous little mountain in their neighbourhood. The city developed on the remnants of an ancient volcano which has been greatly denuded by erosion. A crag and tail formation formed the nucleus

*Arthur's Seat and the Salisbury Crags*

of the settlement. A castle developed on the crag and housing spread down the tail to the boundaries of Holyrood Park, where royalty commandeered the best of the scenery by enclosing Arthur's Seat and Salisbury Crags.

The royal park is open to the public but has its own police force and regulations, including no organised rock climbing, despite Salisbury Crags offering some of the best climbing in the south of Scotland.

A road encircles Arthur's Seat and Salisbury Crags within the park and climbs nearly half way up the mountain on its east flank at Dunsapie Loch. This approach offers a very easy route to the summit over a slope wrinkled with ancient cultivation terraces.

A longer and grander route starts from the entry to the park near the palace and climbs along the top of Salisbury Crags. This route gives memorable views along the precipitous sill edge to Arthur's Seat as well as over Edinburgh. From a col beyond the crags, Arthur's Seat can be reached by a path on the south side of the Guttit Haddie – a fish-shaped scar where flash floods have stripped away the vegetation.

The craggy summit is an outstanding viewpoint for Fife, the Lothians and far off hills to south, west and north. Concrete slabs and iron rings around the trig point are relics of a war-time gun emplacement.

There are numerous routes to this hill and the area repays exploration. A descent can be made to the north along the Lang Rig on the crest of another prominent sill which passes the ruins of St Anthony's Chapel to St Margaret's Loch. The Radical Road is another outstanding route - constructed by unemployed weavers in the 19th century along the base of the Salisbury Crags. This passes Hutton's section at the foot of the crags, where in the 18th century James Hutton made the pioneering geological discovery of a spectacular junction between the igneous and sedimentary rocks.

The bulging basaltic columns of Samson's Ribs should not be missed on the south edge of the park, above the point where a pathway passes by an inclined plane for 600 metres through a tunnel on the former Edinburgh and Dalkeith Railway of 1831.

### Caerketton Hill (478m)
Standing at the northern end of the range so near to Edinburgh, this is the most popular of the Pentlands. The northern crags frown down on the city by-pass and Swanston, where Robert Louis Stevenson spent part of his childhood. Scars of scree known as the Seven Sisters can be seen among the crags from the city. Swanston maintains a peaceful air, but Hillend to the east has been swamped by recreational development.

The Hillend Country Park is a very popular ski centre, on snow when available, and all round the year on artificial slopes. A chair lift, ski tows, access road, car park, restaurant and associated developments line the Lothian Burn. Walkers can soon leave all this behind though, and rise above Hillend Hill to turn west along the ridge to Caerketton Hill.

The route from Swanston starts at a car park beneath a tall house and passes between the attractive cluster of restored 18th century thatched cottages. Climb up the east bank of the burn, cross to the west bank opposite the cross-shaped wood and climb to the col west of the crags. The ridge leads east to two cairns. The eastern one is higher and dates from the Bronze Age. The hill can also be reached from Boghall on the A702. The East of Scotland Agricultural College Farm has a car park for visitors and a farm trail. The track up the Boghall Burn climbs to the col west of the summit.

### Allermuir Hill (493m)
This is a compact hill with a cone shaped summit which carries a trig point, a fence, some MOD bric-a-brac, and a view indicator which looks as far as the Ochil and Tweedsmuir hills and The Cobbler.

The hill can be climbed from Caerketton Hill along the ridge, from Swanston by a path up the north-eastern slopes, or from a footpath to the west between Dreghorn and Castlelaw. The north-western slopes facing this last route are steep and craggy. The south-western ridge offers an easier route with a fence for guidance. Capelaw Hill to the west is a grassy hill crowned with the remains of a flag pole. A track from Glencorse to Bonaly crosses the west side of Capelaw Hill.

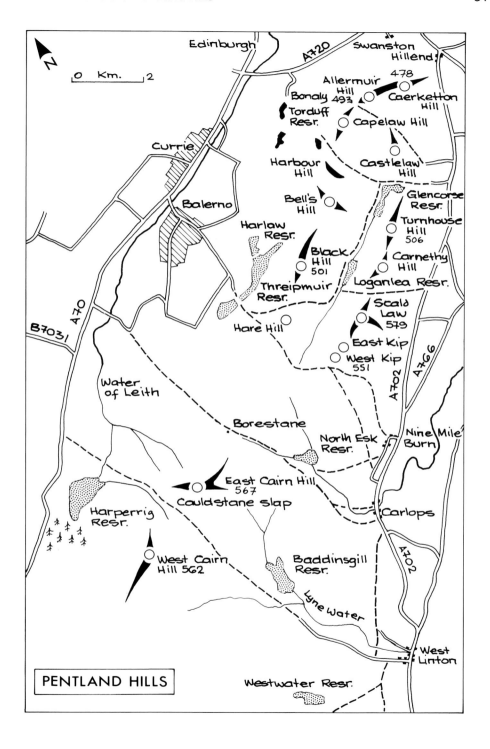

PENTLAND HILLS

*Looking from Allermuir to Carnethy Hill, Scald Law and the Kips*

**Castlelaw Hill** (488m)
The ridge of this hill forms the upright to a T-shaped formation formed with
Caerketton Hill, Allermuir Hill and Capelaw Hill. While Castlelaw Hill is denied
the splendid views to Edinburgh enjoyed by its northern neighbours, it boasts the
best views of hills in the range as it looks south over Glencorse Reservoir into the
heart of the Pentlands.

The hill rises north of Glencorse Reservoir and has a south-facing quarry used
by the MOD as a firing range. Walking is restricted in the area during firing and a
circle of red and white posts round the south face of the hill marks the danger zone.
Red lamps are used to warn of firing after dark, but most restrictions are lifted by
mid-afternoon.

The shortest route to the hill starts from a car park at Castlelaw Farm above the
A702. MOD notices can be misleading in this area as access is unrestricted to the 1st
and 2nd century AD fort and souterrain above the car park which is on a right of
way to Dreghorn. This track is used by MOD vehicles to reach the summit of
Castlelaw Hill from the north. Walkers may do so also and stay just outside the
danger area.

*Glencorse Reservoir from the path between Harbour Hill and Bell's Hill*

### Turnhouse Hill (506m)

This hill sits between the A702 and the Logan Glen at the northern end of the main Pentlands chain. Glencorse Reservoir bends around its northern slopes and is a fine feature in the view from the hill.

An easy and attractive route to the hill starts from the visitor centre at the foot of the Logan Glen near the A702. Walk along the road until clear of the trees and take a track south-westwards along the burn to a bridge or stepping stones. The path rises directly to the hill and passes through a fringe of trees to gain the north ridge.

The view across the reservoir includes the firing range which can disturb the peace! A real battlefield can be seen to the south-east, where at Rullion Green in 1666, below an Iron Age fort, a Covenanter force was routed by General Tam Dalyell. A monument at the east end of a wood above Turnhouse commemorates the event. The summit of Turnhouse Hill carries a cairn and lies about 400 metres south of a grassy north top.

### Carnethy Hill (573m)

This hill lies south-west of Turnhouse Hill and most walkers will include it in a traverse of the chain of hills above the A702. There is an interesting change in vegetation on the north-east ridge. To the north the slopes are grassy and are grazed by sheep. Grass gives way to heather and scree on Carnethy Hill where grouse are more numerous than sheep. A large Bronze Age cairn crowns the summit of the hill, but has been much disturbed.

A quick approach to the hill follows the Kirk Road, which climbs from the A702 north of Silverburn and crosses the col south-west of the hill before descending to The Howe.

### Scald Law (579m)
An advantage of six metres over Carnethy Hill makes this the highest of the Pentland Hills. It is a more complicated hill than its neighbours and needs some care when navigating in mist. It is generally climbed from the north from the Kirk Road or from Carnethy Hill. The summit is smooth with a trig point as the only decoration, while Penicuik is prominent in views to the east.

The alignment of the main ridge follows the usual north-east to south-west direction, but short ridges run out to the south-east from both sides of the summit. The ridge going south-west from Scald Law takes a pronounced bend to the south-east to South Black Hill where there is a substantial cairn. North of the col between this hill and the main summit a not very obvious spur leads down to the west and the continuation of the main ridge. This route passes an erratic boulder just before the col to East Kip showing that ice action has helped to shape the Pentlands.

### West Kip (551m)
A distance of only half a kilometre separates West Kip from the slightly lower East Kip. The Kips are the most shapely peaks in the Pentlands and are often mistaken for Highland cones when seen afar off from the south. They can be reached by a variety of routes, but are usually climbed in a traverse along the main ridge from Turnhouse Hill.

From Nine Mile Burn two routes run in parallel to the col west of West Kip. The higher route heads directly for Cap Law along the Monk's Road and passes the hollowed Font Stone, which may have been a base for a cross shaft. The lower route crosses the Quarrel Burn and the col between Cap Law and Braid Law and joins with the higher route after passing an old wood.

The West Kip has a remarkably narrow ridge and in places it is difficult for two people to pass each other. This short, level, knobbly ridge leads to a col and the steep-sided but more grassy East Kip.

If a traverse of the range has been made from Flotterstone, a descent can be made from East Kip to The Howe to return down the Logan Glen.

### Black Hill (501m)
This is the highest of the hills on the north side of the Logan Glen. It is a rounded, heathery hill and is scarred by a road to its summit from the east for shooters.

The hill can be reached from Balerno by the track which starts south of Threip-muir Reservoir near Bavelaw Castle. This track passes through a glacial meltwater channel known as the Green Cleugh which is well seen from the southern slopes of Black Hill. The remains of Howlet's House sit under the hill above the Loganlea Reservoir and may date from the 16th century.

A traverse of Black Hill, Bell's Hill and Harbour Hill offers an alternative route to the walk along the Logan Glen road but does not have official approval.

### East Cairn Hill (567m)
From the north, the Cauldstane Slap which separates the East and West Cairn Hills is one of the most distinctive landmarks in the Pentlands.

The shortest approach to both hills follows the old drove road from the A70, which starts at a parking place south of Little Vantage and north of Harperrig Reservoir. This crosses a bridge at the Gala Ford, passes east of Harperrig and rises east of the Baad Park Burn to the foot of the west ridge of East Cairn Hill. A path climbs the ridge through zones of heather, blaeberry and boulders to the large ancient cairn on the north-west summit. A curving ridge runs on towards the south-east over the main summit. Walking conditions are soft on this ridge, but the character is relieved by a number of tors jutting from the skyline where the Old Red Sandstone stands clear of the peat. The horizontal bedding of the rocks has supplied abundant building material for the superbly crafted stone walls running along the ridge. One of the dykes descends to the Bore Stane which is an approach route from Balerno or Carlops.

### West Cairn Hill (562m)
The Cauldstane Slap separates this hill from East Cairn Hill. West Cairn Hill is the first distinctive summit seen in the Pentlands when approaching from the west and is also the source of the Water of Leith.

A wall leads the way south-west then west to the summit of this hill from the Cauldstane Slap. Tinto is prominent in views from the trig point to the south-west over rolling moorland. A long ridge extends to the south-west while a short, narrow and rocky ridge offers a short-cut back to Harperrig.

## PATHS AND WALKS

*Glencorse to Balerno, Currie or Bonaly.* This route starts from the A702 and follows the Logan Glen road to the north end of Glencorse Reservoir. A number of variations lead on past the east or south-west sides of Harbour Hill. (7 or 8 kilometres).

*Penicuik to Balerno.* This route leaves the A702 north of Silverburn and crosses the col to The Howe by the Kirk Road. It continues through the pass between Hare Hill and Black Hill to cross Threipmuir Reservoir and join the public road at the Red Moss south of Marchbank Hotel. (10 kilometres).

*The Cauldstane Slap*

*Nine Mile Burn to Balerno.* The start of this route follows either of the two parallel approaches mentioned for West Kip. It then crosses near the source of the Logan Burn to pass west of Hare Hill and descend a fine beech avenue to cross Threipmuir Reservoir. (10 kilometres).

*Carlops to Balerno by the Bore Stane.* A footpath at the north end of Carlops goes up the north bank of the North Esk then crosses to join a road at Fairliehope. This road is left where it turns east and a route is taken between the North Esk Reservoir and the plantation to its west to the Bore Stane. The track then drops northwards to pass east of Listonshiels. An alternative start takes the farm road to Spittal between Carlops and Nine Mile Burn, passes round the east side of the farm and climbs over the col north of Patie's Hill to cross the dam at the North Esk Reservoir and join the first route. (13 kilometres).

*The Cauldstane Slap.* The first part of this route from the A70 was mentioned under East Cairn Hill. From the col between the East and West Cairn hills the route descends southwards past Baddinsgill Reservoir and Baddinsgill Farm where the public road is joined to West Linton. (13 kilometres). A variation can be made on the last section by crossing to the east bank of the Lyne Water at (127 546) and passing Stonypath to a junction which offers routes to West Linton or Carlops.

*Crosswoodburn to Garvald.* Start from the A70 at (051 578) and go along the west side of the plantation west of Crosswood Reservoir. Pass east of Mid Crosswood and between a ruin overlooked by trees on Henshaw Hill and a conspicuous stone man on the rocky White Craig. (A variation joins here from the west after leaving the A70 at the Tarbrax road junction). A track continues along the high ground to Black Law passing a headstone marking the grave of a Covenanter fatally wounded at the Battle of Rullion Green. The descent to the south-east crosses west of Cairn Knowe, or a road from the Darlees Rig can be followed on the west bank of the West Water. If Garvald is your destination, recross the burn lower down. (12 kilometres).

*Lingy Knowe to Dunsyre or West Linton.* This route leaves the A70 seven kilometres north-east of Carnwath and passes through a plantation where a left fork is taken. The route splits again under Left Law with the right branch heading for Dunsyre past Ian Hamilton Finlay's internationally acclaimed sculpture garden at Stonypath. The left branch makes for Medwynhead or the bridge to the north to join a road to West Linton. (7 or 15 kilometres).

*The Water of Leith Trail and the Union Canal.* Walkers with reserves of energy, returning to Edinburgh from the Pentlands, can ignore public transport and join the Water of Leith Trail at Balerno. This follows the route of the former Balerno Branch Railway through Currie and Colinton. Beyond the A70 at Slateford diversions have to be made to link sections of the trail along the river, but walkers can transfer to the tow path on the north bank of the Union Canal, as it passes overhead at Slateford, and continue their walk to Fountainbridge in the city centre. (12 kilometres).

# CHAPTER 6

# The Broughton Heights

| | | |
|---|---|---|
| Penvalla | 537m | 151 396 |
| Ladyurd Hill | 525m | 150 408 |
| Brown Dod | 537m | 135 413 |
| Broughton Heights | 571m | 123 411 |
| Green Law | 560m | 126 405 |
| Clover Law | 493m | 121 390 |
| Trahenna Hill | 549m | 136 374 |

**ACCESS**

The A72 and A701 mark the western frontier of the range, with Broughton on the latter a good base, with a car park at a hall opposite the junction with the B7016 from Biggar. The minor road from Broughton to Dreva and Dawyck passes close to the south end of the range but has parking problems and is not convenient for many of the hills. A circuit of the range is possible from Stobo on the B712 Dawyck to Lyne road and there is parking space beside the restored medieval church if service times are avoided. Ladyurd, off the A72, gives access from the north and a car can be left 100 metres west of the farm road end.

**TRANSPORT**

*Bus:* Edinburgh to Biggar; daily.
Edinburgh to Peebles; daily.
Peebles to Stobo, Drumelzier, Broughton, Biggar and Lanark; Monday to Saturday.
Peebles to Lyne, Blyth Bridge and Carlops; Tuesday and Thursday and schooldays.

**ACCOMMODATION**

Hotels at Broughton, Biggar, Dolphinton and Peebles.

**MAPS**

Ordnance Survey 1:50,000, Sheet 72
Bartholomew 1:100,000, The Borders

The compactness of this range leads to it being overlooked by many walkers. Like many others in eastern Scotland it lacks a loch in its midst to show off its beauty. Nevertheless, it can provide hard exercise and requires some dedication if all the tops are to be visited in one outing. The northern part of the range is forested. Most of the central part is grassy where grazed by sheep, and the southern and eastern parts have a mixture of forest, woodland, farmland and heather moors.

The range takes its name from the highest point of the meandering horseshoe-shaped ridge, where in the north-west it rises higher than several competing summits. The Broughton Heights are possibly the most central of the ranges in the Southern Uplands. The Pentlands lie to the north, the Moorfoots to the north-east, the Tweedsmuir Hills to the south-east, and the Culters to the south-west. The valley of the River Tweed forms an immediate boundary to the south and east, joined by the Lyne Water on the north-east. The Biggar Gap provides an opening to the west with the view down the Clyde valley flanked by Tinto.

The hills are arranged in a straggling chain around the Hopehead Burn, which joins the Weston Burn flowing to the River Tweed through the celebrated parklands and water gardens of Stobo Castle.

The Broughton Heights are equally suited to a number of short expeditions from different points of the compass, or a longer more arduous assault on all the tops. Covering all the high ground involves an ascent of over 1000m and requires very careful planning to eliminate unnecessary climbing and retracing of steps.

A fine view of the range can be had from a footpath which goes from Broughton to Skirling on the A72. This starts at the churchyard above the B7016 and A701. As the path rises westwards, the view back looks to the Broughton Heights rising above the trees, with Broughton Place standing like a sturdy old tower house guarding the gap into the hills. Despite appearances, the house dates from the 1930s and was designed by Basil Spence.

Upper Tweeddale, including the area between Broughton and Lyne has been designated a National Scenic Area by the Countryside Commission for Scotland.

## THE HILLS

### Penvalla (537m)

This heathery hill is the most retiring of the range and is surrounded by hills on three sides and by farmlands and woods to the south. The easiest way to climb the hill on its own starts from the phone box at Stobo and follows a vehicle track on the north side of the Easton Burn to the ruin at Harrowhope. The high path is taken from there through a shelter belt and west to the col south of a fort under Mid Hill. From the cairn on Mid Hill a good view can be had of the fort's defences and the parklands above Stobo Castle.

Penvalla is the higher northern end of the ridge before a 100m descent leads to Ladyurd Hill. If returning to Stobo from Penvalla or Ladyurd Hill, a path on the east side of Harrow Hope can be followed to Harrowhope. If returning to Broughton from a circuit of the range, some loss of height is required to cross the Hopehead valley to the col north of Hammer Head. The path which passes under Mid Hill continues to this col, as does a path passing north of Stobo Hopehead from the col west of Ladyurd Hill.

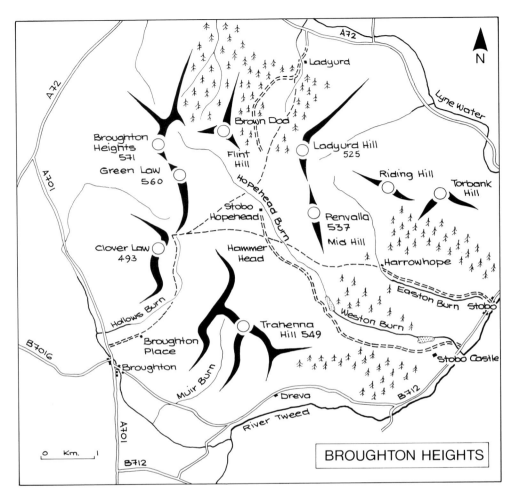

BROUGHTON HEIGHTS

**Ladyurd Hill** (525m)

This hill is easily reached from the north by way of the farm road to Ladyurd from the A72. From the farm, follow a vehicle track going south towards pastures beyond a shelter belt. Take a forest road west along this shelter belt and stay with the road as it curves up the valley under Brown Dod and Flint Hill to the col west of Ladyurd Hill. The forested north-western slopes of Ladyurd Hill are devoid of firebreaks, but a route clear of the plantation leads up the fence from the col to the south end of the summit ridge. The summit is about 400 metres north of there.

A ridge runs eastwards from Ladyurd Hill to Riding Hill (470m) and Torbank Hill (460m). The east end of the latter offers a splendid view down to the Roman fort which stands above Lyne Bridge and the A72.

Summer and winter at Broughton; Trahenna Hill from the path to Skirling

### Brown Dod (537m)

This is the most northerly hill in the group and can be climbed from Ladyurd (see Ladyurd Hill). To reach it from Broughton requires the crossing of the pass between Broomy Side and Hammer Head, where a gate in a fence marks the route down a gully on an indistinct footpath to the foot of Flint Hill. A fence follows the ridge up Flint Hill and over Brown Dod with forest to the east. The view east looks to the Eildons past Lee Pen in the gap of the Tweed valley. There is a gate in a fence in the col west of Brown Dod where a footpath leads north into the forest through a firebreak.

### Broughton Heights (571m)

The highest and most north-westerly hill in the group stands on the edge of the Southern Uplands with an extensive view over the Central Lowlands. The detached character of Tinto and the Pentlands from the Southern Uplands is very obvious from here as they rise above the level plain.

The hill is aligned in a north to south direction, bending north-east to a slight top at Wether Law (557m). Ridges run north-west, north, north-east and south-east from this north top, with an electric fence running along the summit ridge past Broughton Heights. An approach to Broughton Heights from Brown Dod or Green Law avoids the problem of crossing this fence.

### Green Law (560m)

This hill sits north of the Hammer Head pass from which it can be reached on a route from Broughton. A fence leads up from the pass and joins with another from Clover Law on Broomy Side. After two short dips, the ridge reaches Green Law before turning north-west to Broughton Heights.

### Clover Law (493m)

An easy walk from Broughton can gain this summit, which lies inconveniently off the main ridge for those attempting a complete circuit. The route goes up the tree lined avenue to Broughton Place, passing through the sleeping lions gateway and continuing north-eastwards on a green road above the Hollows Burn. Once the road has crossed the burn, the heathery slopes can be climbed to the ridge where a fence runs along the summit. A col to the north-east joins the hill to others in the range.

### Trahenna Hill (549m)

This is the most southerly hill in the range. It can be reached easily from Broughton Place, the Hammer Head pass or the Dreva road. The main ridge runs south-east from the Hammer Head pass, then turns south-west before splitting at the Broughton end into spurs running north-west, west, and south and west. An east ridge runs from the north end of the hill to Hog Knowe (423m), while a south-easterly ridge branches from the centre of the main ridge and rises beyond a col to the main summit before turning south to Dreva. A fence and wall run from Hammer Head along the main ridge and a fence runs south-east to the main summit which is marked by a post and a few stones.

A path leaves the col north-west of the main summit and contours the west side of the Muir Burn's valley before joining the ridge down to Ratchill. Unusually for these hills, this ridge has a few outcrops on it and the vegetation becomes scanty on the descent past some ancient settlement sites.

Hammer Head at the north end of the hill has a wedge shaped outline while the plan of the whole hill can suggest a hammer. A fine view can be had from the southerly ridges of the hill to Broughton and the Tweed valley. The quarry beyond Dreva Wood was once an important supplier of roofing slates.

## PATHS AND WALKS

*Broughton to Stobo.* An old drove road goes from Broughton past Broughton Place and over the Hammer Head pass to cross the Hopehead Burn and cross a col south of Mid Hill. It then drops to Harrowhope and takes the north bank of the Easton Burn to Stobo. (10 kilometres).

# CHAPTER 7

# The Tweedsmuir Hills

| | | |
|---|---|---|
| **Birkscairn Hill** | 661m | 275 332 |
| **Dun Rig** | 743m | 253 316 |
| **Glenrath Heights** | 730m | 242 323 |
| **Stob Law** | 676m | 230 333 |
| **Black Law** | 698m | 223 280 |
| **Greenside Law** | 643m | 198 255 |
| **Pykestone Hill** | 737m | 173 313 |
| **Drumelzier Law** | 668m | 149 312 |
| **Middle Hill** | 716m | 159 294 |
| **Dollar Law** | 817m | 178 278 |
| **Cramalt Craig** | 831m | 168 247 |
| **Broad Law** | 840m | 146 236 |
| **Talla Cleuch Head** | 690m | 133 218 |

The Tweedsmuir or Manor Hills are encircled by the River Tweed on the west and north, and by the Ettrick Water, Yarrow Water, Megget Water and Talla Reservoir on the east and south. The range has the Moorfoots as its northern neighbours while the Culters lie across the Tweed to the west. The Moffat Hills lie to the south of the Talla Reservoir - Megget Reservoir gap, which rises to a col at 452m at the Megget Stone where it is a simple matter to cross from the Tweedsmuir Hills to the Moffat Range.

The higher hills are concentrated in the western section of the Tweedsmuir Hills where there are three of the top five summits in Donald's Tables, including a Corbett. Eastwards the range tends to fall away to merge in lower ground with the Moffat, Ettrick and Border Hills towards Selkirk. The range is essentially a Y-shaped ridge which does not lose much height as it sweeps across the countryside from summit to summit. With numerous Donalds and tops it lends itself to summit bagging on a grand scale for those who like long walks. Against that, there are quite a number of subsidiary ridges bearing separate hills or tops which are time and energy consuming if they have to be collected in a grand sweep. They are more easily reached in circular routes by going up one ridge and down another.

Most of the hills are grouped in a U-shape around the Manor Water Glen which cuts deep into the hills to a col only two kilometres from the Megget Reservoir on

## ACCESS

The A701 Broughton to Tweedsmuir road allows these hills to be visited at bridge points over the River Tweed. A minor road from Tweedsmuir to St Mary's Loch climbs high above Talla reservoir and gives a good start from the south. The A708 from St Mary's Loch to Selkirk moves away from the bigger hills but is still useful. The B709 Gordon Arms to Innerleithen road cuts north through the hills from the A708 but is remote from the Donalds save for one corner of the range near Traquair. Northern approaches start from the A72 in the Peebles-Innerleithen area and cross the River Tweed to the B7062 or minor roads to reach the Manor Glen where a very useful road runs south to near Manorhead in the middle of the range. The B712 running between the A72 and A701 offers starting points at Drumelzier and near Stobo.

## TRANSPORT

*Bus:* Edinburgh to Peebles and Galashiels; daily.
Edinburgh to Tweedsmuir and Dumfries; Friday, Saturday, and Sunday.
Peebles to Drumelzier and Lanark; Monday to Saturday.
Peebles to Gordon Arms and Galashiels; Monday to Friday.

*Postbus:* Biggar to Tweedsmuir and Talla Farm; Monday to Saturday.
Peebles to Manorhead; Monday to Saturday.

## ACCOMMODATION

Hotels at Innerleithen, Walkerburn, Peebles, Broughton, Clovenfords, Selkirk, Yarrow Valley, St Mary's Loch and Tweedsmuir.
Camping at Innerleithen, Peebles, Selkirk and St Mary's Loch.
Youth Hostels at Broadmeadows and Melrose.

## MAPS

Ordnance Survey 1:50,000, Sheets 72 and 73
Bartholomew 1;100,000 The Borders

the southern edge of the range. Writers seem reluctant to use the word glen in connection with the Manor Water and prefer the term valley, reflecting the influences from across the border on the Southern Uplands. Despite Glensax, The Glen, Glenrath and other glens in the range, Glenmanor is not a widely used term. Scenically it is a glen amidst the higher hills and a valley where it opens out to join the Tweed. There is a house called Glenvalley to the east of Dun Rig which well illustrates the mix-up of languages.

# THE HILLS

### Birkscairn Hill (661m)

This is the apex of a V-shaped formation of hills which sends ridges northwards to Peebles and north-east to Innerleithen enclosing the Cardrona Forest. The ridge up from Peebles bears the continuation of the old drove road from the Cauldstane Slap in the Pentlands which is also mentioned under the Moorfoots. This route crosses the River Tweed at Peebles and today follows Springhill Road and Glen Road south-eastwards towards Whitehaugh Farm. The Glensax Burn is crossed south-west of the farm and the track taken uphill between Glensax and Kailzie. It is worth going directly up the ridge for the views before rejoining the drove road which winds between the hillocks. The road is distinctly bounded by two stone walls about fifteen metres apart, but heather has now colonised the route which once would have been worn bare.

The road meets a plantation beyond Kailzie Hill and runs up its west side (having now lost its boundary walls) to Kirkhope Law (536m) where there is a cairn. A fence continues south-west and south to a cairn on Birkscairn Hill. Beyond the cairn the fence drops south-west to a col where a path from St Mary's Loch to Glensax reaches its highest point.

The hill can also be climbed from Glensax, Cardrona Forest or the Quair Water west of the B709.

**Dun Rig** (743m)

This hill sits at the head of Glensax and can be climbed from there by the S-shaped north ridge. It is usually climbed along with others in its group, especially Birkscairn Hill to the north-east. A ruined fence climbs from the Birkscairn Hill col over Stake Law (679m) to Dun Rig. The going is generally soft and peaty underfoot as the route zigzags among the hollows. Three fences meet at a trig point on Dun Rig. To continue the ridge walk to Glenrath Heights, the south-west fence should be followed for about 800 metres before cutting the corner westwards to rejoin the ridge as it bends northwards. The contour across the catchment area for the two head burns of Glensax requires a carefully chosen line among the eroded peat hags, but there is nothing to be gained by taking the longer route along the ridge where the going is just as soft. Three fences meet on the west shoulder of Dun Rig with one continuing north to firmer ground on Glenrath Heights.

TWEEDSMUIR HILLS

Drumelzier Law 668

Pykestone Hill 737

Middle Hill 716

Dollar Law 817

Manorhead

Hunt Low 639

Cramalt Craig 831

Greenside L 64?

Broad Law 840

Clockmore 6

Talla Cleuch Head 690

Tweedsmuir

Talla Reservoir

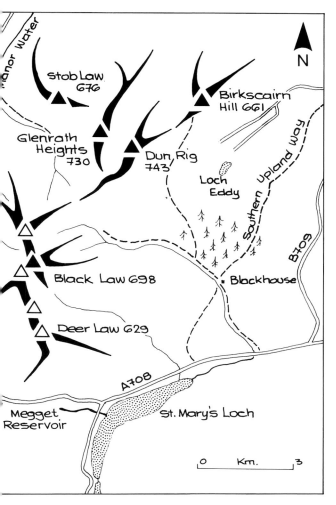

Dun Rig can be climbed from St Mary's Loch at Dryhope using the Southern Upland Way to Blackhouse, or from Craig Douglas farther east on the A708 to the same point. The road up the Douglas Burn is followed for one kilometre beyond Blackhouse then a branch road taken north through the forest on the east side of the Bught Rig. Beyond the end of the road a path continues then splits left to Dun Rig and right for The Glen.

Although the right branch is well off the route to Dun Rig, time should be found for exploring it as well. East of Peat Hill there is a remarkable little canyon, which twists about before opening out as a glacial meltwater channel to Loch Eddy and its island in a spectacular setting of pines, heather and steep rocky slopes.

### Glenrath Heights (730m)

The summit of this hill sits at the southern end of a two kilometre-long ridge which runs southwest from Hundleshope Heights (685m) along the western side of Glensax. Glenrath runs west from Glenrath Heights to join the Manor Glen.

The hill can best be climbed from Glenrath Farm near the meeting of the two waters by following the private road up the glen to Glenrathope and ascending the west ridge. A fence runs up from the west shoulder of Dun Rig to the heathery slopes of Glenrath Heights and continues northwards to Broom Hill, where one branch goes west towards Stob Law and another continues along the main ridge to Hundleshope Heights.

The view from the ridge can include The Cheviot, the Eildons, Ben Lomond and Stuc a' Chroin, while Salisbury Crags, Arthur's Seat and the East Lomond are in line through the Eddleston gap.

*Talla Reservoir from the slopes of Talla Cleuch Head*

The extensive northern slopes of Hundleshope Heights have been eaten into by a number of burns giving a choice of at least five ridges between Glensax and the Cademuir trench to follow to the summit. From Upper Newby in Glensax a north-east ridge climbs over a distinctive wedge-shaped top at Newby Kipps to Preston Law. This ridge gives a good view of a ring fort on the neighbouring ridge across the Waddenshope Burn.

### Stob Law (676m)
This hill is generally climbed along with Glenrath Heights. If the round of Glensax is being done, Stob Law requires a diversion across a col at 600m. From the Manor Glen, the hill is easily reached from Glenrath by the west shoulder or southern slopes which are heathery and broken with scree. There is a small cairn at the summit and a fence runs east to west along the main ridge to Glenrath Hill where a long northerly ridge runs down over Canada Hill to Cademuir.

On the lower slopes of the hill, north of the Glenrath Burn, there is an extensive area of ancient settlements and field systems, with cultivation terraces, boundary walls and clearance cairns predating the modern dykes and stells.

## Black Law (698m)

This high ridge separates Manorhead from St Mary's Loch. It is a rather featureless hill running from south-west to north-east with both ends of the one kilometre long summit ridge rising slightly to vie for supremacy. Donald's Tables originally gave the honour to the south-west top, but new maps now make the north-east top very slightly higher. Beyond the summit the ridge drops in a northerly direction with a slight rise before another top called Blackhouse Heights.

A north-west ridge runs down to the Manor Glen from this top while a north-east ridge follows a tedious but elevated route to Dun Rig. The fence from Dun Rig is continuous over Black Law to Redsike Head. A narrow band of ridges and furrows runs parallel with the fence along Black Law.

The hill may be climbed from the end of the road up the Manor Glen by following the path to Redsike Head and turning up the south-west ridge. This path can also be followed to the same point from the Megget Reservoir. A return on this side can be made over the grassy tops of Conscleuch Head and Deer Law with a fence for company. Conscleuch Head has a cairn at its north end but the summit is farther south. Deer Law's summit is marked by a few boulders west of the fence. Some of the boulders have cup marks on them which may be a result of natural erosion. It is worth finishing a walk in this direction by going over Henderland Hill (531m) and Capper Law (515m) for superb views of Megget Reservoir and St Mary's Loch.

A road from Craig Douglas on the A708 east of St Mary's Loch goes past Blackhouse and Muttonhall all the way to the Long Grain under Blackhouse Heights. A firebreak leads up heather from the road-end, while a branch of this road zigzags up the Whitegrain Rig.

## Greenside Law (643m)

From the end of the public road up the Manor Glen, the view looks south past a widening of the glen at Manorhead to a very distinctive headwall blocking the route to the south and featuring this hill. The glen narrows dramatically from a U-shape at Manorhead to steep V-shaped cleuchs on either side of Greenside Law. That to the east of the north ridge contains a number of dome-shaped protuberances - suggestive of land-slip formations perhaps more than drumlins. The plateau-like expanses of the Tweedsmuir Hills have been bitten into in this area by erosion. The ridge between Greenside Law and Shielhope Head has been scoured to a narrow col which forms a watershed between two of the River Tweed's tributaries which flow in opposite directions.

The right of way track from the car park north of Manorhead to Megget Reservoir makes a good line of ascent to this hill. A fence leads from the highest point of the track on Black Rig to the grassy summit of Greenside Law.

## Pykestone Hill (737m)

From the B712 at Drumelzier, a road runs a short distance up the Drumelzier Burn as far as a hall where cars may be left. A track continues through the fields and by the tree-lined burn, crossing it just past its junction with the Scrape Burn. Continue with the track uphill between two blocks of larch and pine to Den Knowes Head and on to the summit of Pykestone Hill, where a trig point sits by the fence running between Long Grain Knowe and The Scrape.

The Thief's Road from Dawyck Mill skirts the east side of The Scrape, Pykestone Hill and Long Grain Knowe on its route to Dollar Law and Megget. The route to Pykestone Hill from Drumelzier follows a branch of this track.

A return to Drumelzier from Pykestone Hill can be made over Drumelzier Law or by The Scrape and Scawd Law. This last route has an interesting finish with a steep scree run from two prominent cairns above Drumelzier to an ancient fort and the remains of Tinnis Castle on a boulder-strewn little ridge above the flood plain of the River Tweed.

### Drumelzier Law (668m)
A little fin at the south-east end of the summit ridge gives this hill a distinctive shape when seen from a number of directions. The hill juts out boldly from the main chain of Tweedsmuir Hills and makes it a splendid viewpoint for the Tweed valley, the Culters and the plains of Strathclyde.

Drumelzier Law is easily climbed from the A701 crossing the River Tweed by a bridge opposite the north-west ridge (124 322). This ridge is heathery but beyond the summit cairn the ground becomes stony where the ridge takes on its familiar wedge shape. The heather reasserts itself lower down.

### Middle Hill (716m)
This summit forms part of a curious H-shaped height between Pykestone Hill and Dollar Law, with rises on each arm of the H. It is not clear how the hill gets its name, though it could be considered the mid summit of a round of the ridge from Taberon Law to Drumelzier Law.

Middle Hill can be reached from the A701 at Stanhope. There is a layby north of the bridge over the River Tweed. The vehicle track along the north side of the Stanhope Burn gives access to the scree slopes of Craig Head, or heather and bracken slopes farther east leading to Taberon Law (637m). The fence running along the ridge continues to Middle Hill across a slight dip, passing a stone man on the south side of the col. The summit of Middle Hill is marked by a few stones on the south-east side of the fence.

Another route from the same bridge goes north to Hopecarton and takes a forest road which runs directly up the south side of the Hopecarton Burn (with branches to right and left) climbing high to the head of the glen just below Taberon Law and Middle Hill.

Glenstivon Dod (688m) north of Middle Hill carries a tall well-built stone man marking the change in direction of the ridge to the north-west. Above the col on the Glenstivon Dod side of the ridge to Drumelzier Law there is a conspicuous cairn of large white quartzite boulders which is easily seen from the A701.

*Looking from Drumelzier Law to Tinto*

### Dollar Law (817m)

This ranks fifth in height in Donald's Tables. It sits just west of the upper Manor Glen and is easily climbed from the car park at the end of the road. It can also be reached from the A701 at Stanhope or from Megget Reservoir.

The Manor Glen approach is by far the shortest and most popular. The slopes south of the plantation lead directly and steeply to the summit. A useful path leads up the slope but trends to the south of the hill. A trig point marks the summit where three fences meet on short, firm turf.

Fifescar Knowe (808m) is a slightly lower top one kilometre south of the main summit. A fence and dyke, widely spaced, run parallel between Dollar Law and this top in the manner of a drove road. The authentic drove road, known as the Thief's Road, crosses the col at a gate between the summits in a north-west to south-east direction, having run round Dollar Law from Newholm Hill. Newholm Hill is only a small rise between Long Grain Knowe and Dollar Law, but would be a significant col for weary travellers crossing from four directions, which may explain the array of cairns there.

The descent to Manorhead down the east ridge of Fifescar Knowe looks across the Ugly Grain to a terraced slope on Dollar Law caused by soil creep, and to a fine

*Looking up the Manor Glen to Dollar Law*

prospect down the Manor Glen with the little hillock at Posso a curious glacial obstruction.

The ridge continues south from Fifescar Knowe for 1200 metres to Dun Law, then turns south-west to a high col under Cramalt Craig. If continuing round the head of the Manor Glen, leave the ridge south of Fifescar Knowe where the dyke and fence come together and follow another fence at right angles to the main fence, heading south-east to Notman Law (734m). There is a distinct rise at this point though it is not a Donald top. A steep descent to the south-east leads to another levelling off and rise at Shielhope Head (613m) which also fails to qualify as a top.

In the forest north-east of Dollar Law at (198 290) there is a cairn to Professor John Veitch, a local poet and historian. North of the forest is a 'Font Stone' which was the base of a cross brought to the site. Near it stands a cross marking the supposed site of an ancient chapel.

### Cramalt Craig (831m)
This is the third highest hill in the Southern Uplands. It is a grassy hill with smooth outlines over most of its bulk save for the steeper broken slopes of Little Craig on its south-east.

*Taberon Law and Dollar Law from Stanhope in the Tweed Valley*

*On Broad Law, looking east*

The shortest route to the hill starts from the Megget Reservoir and climbs the south-east ridge by Clockmore and Pykestone Knowe with rewarding views of the reservoir and St Mary's Loch. A fuller day can take in Dollar Law or Broad Law as well, returning by another of the ridges leading to Megget.

The ascents of Cramalt Craig from Broad Law or Dollar Law along the main ridge are gradual with a fence for guidance to the summit cairn. If the three hills are done together, a return across Cramalt Craig can pass some distance below the summit on the west to avoid unnecessary climbing.

## Broad Law (840m)
This is the second highest hill in the Southern Uplands, losing to Merrick by only three metres. The hill stands north of the watershed between Talla and Megget reservoirs and can be reached easily from the Megget Stone at the summit of the road between them. A fence leads uphill from the stone over Fans Law and turns north to leave the stonier steeps for a straightforward grassy approach to the summit from Cairn Law. The summit is marked by a small cairn and trig point at the fence which continues to Cramalt Craig. A strange bandstand-like rotunda sits just north of the summit and is a prominent landmark in the Borders.

The height of this hill and its central position make it an important tracking point for aircraft using the air-lanes. The Broad Law Beacon helps to keep them on course but has rather disfigured the summit cap with its buildings, masts, electrical supply, service road and marker poles. The service road runs up the north-west side of the hill from Hearthstane.

The summit ridge bends to the north-east with a slight drop and rise again and is followed by a branch of the road. A stone wall crosses this ridge and meets this road at an angle and gate. The north summit is a better viewpoint as Megget Reservoir and St Mary's Loch can be seen to the east with the Eildons beyond. A steep grassy descent by the fence leads north-east to the col to Cramalt Craig. A purple cirque of scree and boulders known as the Polmood Craig cuts into the northern slope, while a riven area of peat hags to the south of the col is known as Tods Knowe.

## Talla Cleuch Head (690m)
This hill rises steeply above Talla Reservoir on its north bank. It is not named on the 1:50,000 map where the lower Mathieside Cairn (664m) is shown 500 metres north-west of the main summit. From the south end of the main summit a west ridge falls steeply to the reservoir by Muckle Side. A west ridge falls less steeply from Mathieside Cairn by Middle Dod, but steepens lower down where it runs into the edge of a forest. The steep, grassy slopes should present no problems in dry, summer weather, but need care at all times. The hill is usually climbed along with Broad Law from which it is a gentler ascent by way of Cairn Law. This route gives a spectacular view down the rocky cleuch to Talla Linnfoots, but many fine viewpoints can be found to the reservoir and its neighbourhood along the southern slopes of the hill.

# PATHS AND WALKS

*The Minchmoor.* This historic route leaves the B709 at Traquair and climbs eastwards through forest to pass north of Minch Moor (567m), which can be reached by a short diversion. It continues over Hare Law then drops to Broadmeadows on the Yarrow Water. (11 kilometres).

A longer high-level variation continues from Hare Law over Brown Knowe and the north side of Broomy Law to Three Brethren (464m) where the three tall cairns are boundary markers. The path then drops to Yair on the River Tweed. This route from Traquair is part of the Southern Upland Way. (14 kilometres).

*Peebles to the Manor Water.* From the south side of Tweed Bridge in Peebles this route goes west along Caledonian Road and south by Edderston Road to a gate and footpath going south-west over the ridge of Cademuir Hill. A road on the south side of the hill leads west to the Manor Water, or back to Peebles around the hill by either side. The hill sits like an island between the River Tweed, Manor Water and an almost dry valley to the south and east, which may have been a route for the Manor Water once. The hill is an excellent viewpoint and bears the remains of several forts and settlement sites. (5 kilometres).

*Yarrow to Traquair.* The tall war memorial by the A708 (354 277) marks the start of this walk. From the north-east side of the memorial the route goes west-north-west through the fields and up Blackgrain Rig passing through a series of gates in electric fences. A veer to north-west takes the track to a col west of Welshie Law and a descent to Hannel. The hill north of this ruin is turned on the east for a very scenic descent to Damhead at Traquair. (9 kilometres).

# CHAPTER 8

# The Moffat Hills

| | | |
|---|---|---|
| **Swatte Fell** | 728m | 118 113 |
| **Hart Fell** | 808m | 114 136 |
| **Whitehope Heights** | 636m | 096 139 |
| **Under Saddle Yoke** | 745m | 143 126 |
| **Cape Law** | 721m | 132 150 |
| **Garelet Dod** | 690m | 126 173 |
| **Erie Hill** | 689m | 124 187 |
| **White Coomb** | 822m | 163 151 |
| **Molls Cleuch Dod** | 784m | 151 180 |
| **Lochcraig Head** | 800m | 167 176 |

## ACCESS

Three roads bind this compact range in a triangle: the A701 from Tweedsmuir to Moffat on the west; the A708 from Moffat to St Mary's Loch on the south-east; and the minor road from St Mary's Loch to Tweedsmuir on the north. Minor roads within the triangle lead north from Moffat to Newton on the River Annan and Moffat Well on the Birnock Water, and south from Tweedsmuir to the Fruid Reservoir dam.

## TRANSPORT

*Bus:* Glasgow to Moffat and Dumfries; daily.
Edinburgh to Moffat and Dumfries; Friday, Saturday and Sunday.
Carlisle to Lockerbie and Moffat; daily.
Moffat to Bodesbeck; schooldays.
Melrose to Moffat and St Mary's Loch; Tuesday and Thursday (July to September).

*Postbus:* Biggar to Talla Farm and Fruid; Monday to Saturday.

## ACCOMMODATION

Hotels at Beattock, Moffat, Tweedsmuir and St Mary's Loch.
Camping at Beattock, Moffat and St Mary's Loch.

## MAPS

Ordnance Survey 1:50,000, Sheets 72, 78 and 79
Bartholomew 1:100,000, The Borders

*In the Moffat Water valley, looking towards Bodesbeck Law*

The Moffat Hills are the first range of uplands to make an impression on many north-bound travellers crossing the border. The deep gullies riven into Hart Fell give travellers on the A74 and A701 a distant first taste of the wilder side of Scotland as they follow the Annan Valley along the western boundary of the range. Should they venture along the narrow Moffat-Selkirk road by the Moffat Water on the south-east side of the hills they will gain a much closer impression of the heights towering above, and a respect for the steep, craggy nature of the district. But by crossing the high road between Megget and Talla in the north, road-users join in the grandeur and can enjoy a mountain experience rarely offered without hard physical effort. The district is deservedly popular with tourists and Moffat is a very busy little stopping-off town on longer journeys.

The major hills of the area are grouped in chains towards the south-east above the Moffat Water with ridges running northwards to the three reservoirs at Fruid, Talla and Megget. There are two Corbetts in the range and the ten Donalds listed in this chapter can be combined with the thirteen Tweedsmuir Donalds across the 452m-high Megget Stone col to form the largest area of uplands in southern Scotland.

The hills are pleasantly grassy in the main and are easy to walk, but some of the slopes are remarkably steep. The area exhibits some of the best examples of corrie formation in the Southern Uplands and there is a Highland quality about some of

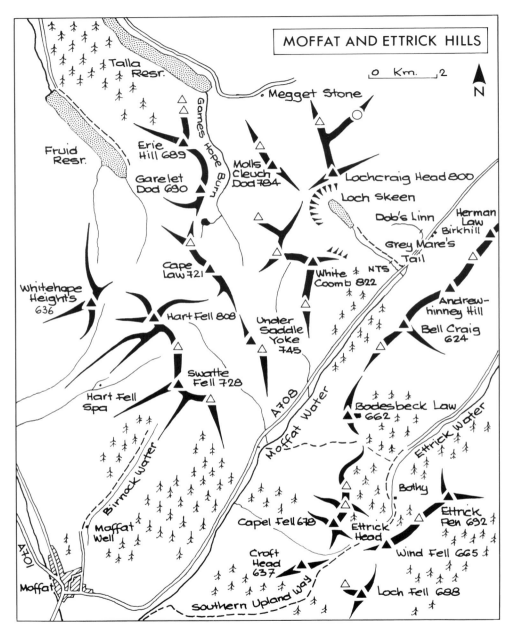

MOFFAT AND ETTRICK HILLS

0 Km. 2

N

Talla Resr.

Megget Stone

Fruid Resr.

Games Hope Burn

Erie Hill 689

Garelet Dod 690

Molls Cleuch Dod 784

Lochcraig Head 800

Loch Skeen

Dob's Linn

Herman Law

Birkhill

Grey Mare's Tail

White Coomb 822

NTS

Cape Law 721

Whitehope Heights 636

Hart Fell 808

Under Saddle Yoke 745

Andrew-hinney Hill

Bell Craig 624

Swatte Fell 728

A708

Moffat Water

Bodesbeck Law 662

Ettrick Water

Hart Fell Spa

Birnock Water

Bothy

Ettrick Pen 692

Moffat Well

Capel Fell 678

Ettrick Head

Wind Fell 665

A701

Croft Head 637

Southern Upland Way

Loch Fell 688

Moffat

the glens and crags. Even where the hills are not broken with outcrops, some prudence is required in descending some of the steeper grass slopes, especially overlooking Moffat Water and the Games Hope Burn. Even where the valleys seem V-shaped, beware of steeper ground lower down where the glaciers have truncated the slopes.

*Looking down the gorge of the Grey Mare's Tail to the Moffat Water*

Loch Skeen exhibits some of the finest character in Southern Uplands scenery. It is a moraine-impounded lake surrounded by frowning crags from which the Tail Burn flows to join with the Midlaw Burn and plunge from a hanging valley about 150m to the Moffat Water below. The Grey Mare's Tail waterfall at this spot is a long white plume about 60m high which can be enjoyed from the car park at its foot. The path on the west goes to the foot of the falls. The path on the east goes to the top and requires care as the ground is very steep and a number of fatalities have occurred there. Fixed belays are in place for rescue work.

Another impressive waterfall in the same area is much less well known as it cannot be seen from the A708. Dob's Linn can be visited from the Grey Mare's Tail car park by walking up the A708 to the bridge over Raking Gill. The linn will be found in the gully to the north and is also a spectacular piece of scenery as two burns from Watch Knowe and Bran Law combine to tumble over a buttress. A legend states that two Covenanters threw the devil over the linn. The gullies here are rich in fossils.

The Grey Mare's Tail and the ground beyond to Loch Skeen and White Coomb were purchased by the National Trust for Scotland in 1962. The area is noted for its wild flowers as well as its scenery and also contains a herd of feral goats.

*Nether Coomb Craig and Swatte Fell from Saddle Yoke*

## THE HILLS

### Swatte Fell (728m)

Swatte Fell is a plateau hill with grassy slopes inclined gently to the west and a steep broken face to the east on which two coombs or corrie-like depressions are separated by a slight ridge. Few crags of size are present as the rock disintegrates fairly quickly and is channelled down gullies to spread as grey fans of scree across the lower slopes.

The Birnock Water on the south side and the Auchencat Burn on the north-west have cut back into the plateau forming a south-west ridge between them. The plateau narrows in the north to a ridge leading to a top above Falcon Craig; in the south it bends eastwards to a top above Nether Coomb Craig where an airy little saddle runs out to a small spur above a long straight gully.

The most direct approach to the hill is from Capplegill on the A708. The ground is steep but the views are good to Moffat Dale. Once Nether Coomb Craig's top is reached, a path leads on round the rim of the coomb past a small lochan to the summit at a dyke which runs from the south-west ridge to the north ridge. Several points on the plateau can claim to be the summit, but the official spot is to the west.

The hill can also be climbed from Moffat Well by following a forest road past Blaebeck up the Birnock Water. This ends at a gate onto open slopes directly under the three clefts known as Birnock Cloves which lead up to near the summit. A return can be made by following a fence and dyke along the ridge above the forest to Blue Cairn and Greygill Head.

**Hart Fell** (808m)
This is the seventh highest Donald in the Southern Uplands. It can be climbed from the A701, Fruid Reservoir, the A708, or the minor road from Moffat to Newton.

The hill stands up boldly as a broad, grassy, gully-indented whale-back when seen from the west, but erosion has taken huge bites out of its eastern flanks leaving steep, craggy faces above the Black Hope.

The most direct approach to the hill starts from south of Newton where a right of way sign points to Hart Fell Spa. Follow the path through fields and up the Auchencat Burn to a split in the glen. Take the north branch and the spa is soon found at burn level near the entrance to a defile which is conspicuous from the A701 because of its black shale and silvery screes.

The mineral quality of the water was discovered by John Williamson, a mining engineer working in the glen in 1748. While most pilgrims to Moffat for health in the 18th and 19th centuries visited the more accessible Moffat Well nearer the town, others made regular expeditions to the Hartfell Spa to take the water. The chalybeate water, if not the exercise, was thought to cure ailments, but its appearance and taste are off-putting.

To continue to Hart Fell it is better to backtrack slightly and climb onto either ridge above the Spa Well Burn. The adventurous may continue up the ravine, scrambling over boulders to the grassy exit to the burn's source but the route is rather precarious, undercut in places, threatened with landslips in others, and bounded by steep scree slopes and shattered rocks. As a spectacle the glen is well worth a visit, but care is needed.

The ridges flanking the spa come together to form Arthur's Seat, the south-west ridge of Hart Fell. A path up this joins a fence to lead to the summit. Three fences meet where the trig point stands within a crescent windbreak of stones.

Those coming from the A708 can climb directly from the Black Hope avoiding the crags, or can cross from Swatte Fell and Falcon Craig following a fence up the south-east ridge. The fence down the north ridge points to Fruid Reservoir and should be left on a north-west course by those heading for Whitehope Heights or the A701 above the Devil's Beef Tub.

The round of the Black Hope over Swatte Fell, Hart Fell and Saddle Yoke makes a good outing from the A708 at Capplegill. A fence can be followed from Hart Fell running north-east and east to Hartfell Rig. When the fence turns north-east and descends to a peat-scarred area south of Cape Law, it is time to lose some height and cross the Whirly Gill.

*Whitehope Heights and Hart Fell from the west*

### Whitehope Heights (636m)

When looking across the Annan valley from the A701 as you climb out of Moffat, this hill and its lower top to the south-east show as shapely cones to the side of Hart Fell.

Whitehope Heights is the highest point on the great amphitheatre surrounding the headwaters of the Annan, until Hart Fell rises as a great watershed between the Annan and Moffat waters' tributaries. The A701 rises to 390m at the west end of this amphitheatre and gives a high start for the hill though Annanhead Hill, Great Hill and Chalk Rig Edge are elevations in the way which have to be climbed or contoured. The first course is better since the views are fine to the Annan valley and the spectacular drop to the Devil's Beef Tub, where stolen cattle were hidden, and a fugitive is said to have folded himself in his plaid and rolled down the steep slope like a ball to escape from his captors.

A path descending to Corehead from the col between Annanhead Hill and Great Hill gives a sensational view to the Beef Tub. A monument above the Beef Tub commemorates a Covenanter shot there, while another monument to the west on the A701 records the perishing in a snowstorm in 1831 of the driver and guard of the Dumfries to Edinburgh mail coach.

A boundary fence or dyke follows the high ground over Annanhead Hill to Chalk Rig Edge. Whitehope Heights has no fence or cairn, but the summit is about 500 metres south-west of the 614m spot height on the map which marks the north-east end of a well-defined ridge.

## Under Saddle Yoke (745m)

Two of the most distinctive peaks in the Southern Uplands are Under Saddle Yoke and its near neighbour Saddle Yoke. They rise steeply from the glens and are joined high up by a neat, narrow saddle. Saddle Yoke has a pointed peak shape when seen from most directions, while the slightly higher Under Saddle Yoke has more of a platform summit as its peak has been lopped near the top.

The slopes are very steep and grassy mostly, for, unlike the other hills in this area, they have weathered fairly uniformly and do not show the same amount of crags as those around. Nevertheless, the effects of weather, erosion and gravity are seen on the north-east slopes where the thin vegetation shows a remarkable fluted pattern.

The ascent of the peaks is quickly achieved by the south ridge from Capplegill on the A708. From a track heading up the north side of the Blackhope Burn, a path goes through a gate in a fence onto the south ridge. There is a small drop beyond a hillock at 490m then the ridge rises steadily to a cairn just south of the highest point of Saddle Yoke. A drop of 30m to the saddle leads to the ascent to Under Saddle Yoke. A traverse of these summits can offer a stimulating walk in winter conditions, but proper equipment and great care are needed on icy slopes and a possibly corniced ridge.

Beyond Under Saddle Yoke a broad north ridge leads at an easy angle to cols leading to White Coomb and Hart Fell. Ridge walks round the Black Hope or Carrifran Burn are popular.

## Cape Law (721m)

The remoteness of this cone-shaped hill is probably its greatest distinction. It is somewhat farther away from the nearest public road than the other Donalds in the range, but it is still a fairly easy expedition. It can be climbed from Fruid, Talla or the A708 at Capplegill. The last route ascends the Blackhope Burn and Whirly Gill to the long south-east ridge leading to Cape Law. A dyke and fence run on to a north-west top, Din Law, and further north to Garelet Dod. Din Law is quite stony and looks down the length of Fruid Reservoir.

## Garelet Dod (690m)

This hill rises in a sweeping ridge from Fruid and may be ascended by walking the length of the reservoir from the dam and going straight up Strawberry Hill to the summit. This route enjoys an uninterrupted view of the reservoir. From the summit at the west end of the ridge a dyke and fence lead on southwards over Ellers Cleuch Rig and down to a rocky breach in the ridge west of the lonely Gameshope Loch. The loch feeds Talla down the Games Hope Burn but may possibly have had an exit west to the Fruid Water at one time. The fence and dyke here are continuous from Din Law over Garelet Dod and north to Erie Hill.

*White Coomb from Loch Skeen*

### Erie Hill (689m)
This hill lies about two kilometres south of the east end of Talla Reservoir and can be reached best from Talla Linnfoots. A ridge, forested on the west, runs south from the reservoir over two tops - Garelet Hill and Lairds Cleuch Rig to the summit.

The ascent from Talla Linnfoots to Garelet Hill is steep and unrelenting but can be rewarded with a magnificent view along the reservoir to the Culter hills. Talla Linnfoots is seen below sitting on the depositional plain from which the road throws itself at the steep V-shaped pass leading to Megget. The Talla Water tumbles in cataracts beside the road to link up with the maturer but just as impressive Games Hope Burn coming from the south. Burns running east from Garelet Hill have cut neatly through moraines to join the Games Hope Burn.

A trig point sits at the summit of Garelet Hill, with a fence and dyke on its west running south to cross to the east side of Laird's Cleuch Rig and continue past Erie Hill with a branch at right angles leading up to the small cairn at the summit.

### White Coomb (822m)
The name for this hill comes from its south-east facing corrie which tends to hold snow well through the springtime. The hill can be recognised by this cirque of snow from many other hills, but the corrie is not easily seen from the A708 because of the steepness of the ground above and the forestry plantations which cloak the slope.

White Coomb is the highest hill of the range and number four in altitude in the Southern Uplands. Despite this, it is a short expedition on its own from the Grey Mare's Tail car park and is usually visited along with other summits. From the Grey Mare's Tail the route follows the east bank path until the Tail Burn can be crossed and a way made up the rough east ridge to the small cairn marking the flattish summit. A return can be made in a horseshoe-shaped route following the high ground round Loch Skeen.

*The Grey Mare's Tail*

White Coomb can also be reached from the A708 farther west by climbing a firebreak through the trees from Polmoodie to join the south ridge to Carrifran Gans (748m). Easy grassy slopes lead on past a lochan in a col to the north and up to White Coomb.

Firthope Rig (801m) can be reached down the broad westerly ridge by following the remains of a dyke, which rises 30m to join a north-south dyke just to the north of the cairn on this top. At the cairn walkers have the option of going west and south to Rotten Bottom and returning to the A708 over Under Saddle Yoke, or going north to Donald's Cleuch Head and round Loch Skeen. Great Hill to the west of Donald's Cleuch Head is an unimpressive grassy top sitting off the main ridge, but the view from Gameshope below is more impressive. A small hut sits at the foot of the west ridge of Great Hill on the banks of the Games Hope Burn.

A level stretch of broad ridge, with a wall for company, leads north-north-east from Donald's Cleuch Head to Firthybrig Head where wall and ridge turn north-west to Molls Cleuch Dod and another dyke leads east to Talla Nick and the climb to Lochcraig Head. An alternative return misses out the round of Loch Skeen and goes east before Firthybrig Head and over a rise and down the narrow ridge to the south-west shore of Loch Skeen. The Tail Burn can be crossed under normal conditions at the outlet from the loch.

**Molls Cleuch Dod** (784m)
Sitting midway between Talla Reservoir and Loch Skeen, this hill is the summit of a well-defined ridge which runs north-west from the White Coomb plateau. A steep line of ascent starts from Talla Linnfoots and climbs to Carlavin Hill (736m) by the north-west ridge, or an easier slope can be taken by driving up the road to a car park west of the Megget Stone and tackling the north side of the hill. The views can be superb from the slopes of Carlavin Hill, looking to the Games Hope or the vast expanses of the reservoirs at Talla and Megget.

A wall runs over the summit of Carlavin Hill and on across a col to the broader summit of Molls Cleuch Dod. By continuing to the south-east with the wall, the main ridge can be joined at Firthybrig Head.

If returning to Talla by the Games Hope beware of the steep slopes west of Carlavin Hill. The views here are good but the descent is not easy. Games Hope is a very rugged ice-scoured glen. Its house is ruinous and has an unusual pentagonal-sided sheep ree, while Gameshope Castle is a rocky boss by the river above the house. A private road has been constructed with much labour from Talla Linnfoots to the house, but it has to twist among moraines, ice-scored boulders and fractured debris at the side of a tumbling burn in a landscape worthy of the Highlands.

**Lochcraig Head** (800m)
This hill sits midway between the Megget Stone and the Grey Mare's Tail. The routes from both directions are well worth doing, but initially the choice has to be made between the high start of the former or the grandeur of the latter. The Megget Stone is a small monolith at the summit of the road marking the district and former county

*The approach to Hart Fell from the south-west*

boundary. There is a car park on the Talla side of the Megget Stone from which a slight descent is made to a track going up the Talla Water until a slope is chosen to Nickies Knowe. Numerous drumlins in the upper glen can be seen from this top.

Once on the ridge the going is good on easy grassy slopes. Fences from the north-west and north-east ridges join on Talla East Side and run as one to Lochcraig Head where they meet a wall and fence running along the top of the very steep face above Loch Skeen. A small cairn sits south of the wall, but a rise farther north is the summit.

The route from the A708 can give magnificent views as it climbs the path east of the Grey Mare's Tail and wends its way among the glaciated scenery of Loch Skeen. A moraine called The Causey, by a fence east of Loch Skeen, avoids the worst of the boggy low ground and leads to the steeper ground south-east of the summit.

# CHAPTER 9

# The Ettrick Hills

| | | |
|---|---|---|
| Herman Law | 614m | 214 157 |
| Andrewhinney Hill | 677m | 198 139 |
| Bell Craig | 624m | 187 129 |
| Bodesbeck Law | 662m | 170 103 |
| Capel Fell | 678m | 164 069 |
| Croft Head | 637m | 153 056 |
| Loch Fell | 688m | 170 047 |
| Wind Fell | 665m | 179 061 |
| Ettrick Pen | 692m | 200 077 |

This is a large sparsely populated area on the southern edge of the Southern Uplands which is seldom if ever visited by most Scots. Bounded on the west and north by Annandale, Moffatdale, Yarrow and the Ettrick Forest and on the east by the A7 Hawick to Langholm road, the area has no clear cut southern boundary, nor can it be truly classed as mountain territory save for the cluster of Donalds in the north-west. Nevertheless it contains a vast territory for those in search of solitude or new adventures.

The roads, valleys and drainage system of the region are all related. The Yarrow, Ettrick, Borthwick and Teviot waters flow northwards to join the Tweed heading for the North Sea. Heading in the opposite direction, and again running with the north-east to south-west grain of the uplands, are the Moffat, Wamphray and Dryfe waters. The White Esk and Black Esk combine as the River Esk on an independent south-easterly course but ultimately have to conform and turn for the Solway Firth also.

St Mary's Loch in the north of the sector is the largest natural loch in the eastern half of southern Scotland. There are few lochs of any size on this side of the country, but St Mary's stretches in tandem with the smaller Loch of the Lowes. This smaller loch was once part of a larger St Mary's but the two were separated by the deposition of sediments from burns running at right angles into St Mary's.

The fifteen Donalds and tops clustered around the Ettrick valley give this area an appeal for hillwalkers, especially as most can be visited in one long walk. Forests cover large tracts of the region now, and the monotony of much of the silviculture does little to show off the appeal of the lower countryside. As much of the region is

**ACCESS**
The most useful roads for hillwalkers are the A708 Moffat to the Gordon Arms Hotel road running north-west of the main chain of the Ettrick Hills and the road on the south-east of this chain which runs up the Ettrick Valley nearly to Potburn from the B709 at Ettrick. The B709 from the Gordon Arms Hotel to Eskdalemuir divides this region in two from north to south with all the high hills to the west. The B723 running south-west from Eskdalemuir provides a boundary to the south of the higher hill zone but access points are remote from the summits here. The A74 encloses the hill zone in the west, but numerous minor roads lie east of this and link with the road up the Wamphray water to Laverhay which gives a southern approach to the hills. In the east between the B709 and the A7 Langholm to Hawick road there are no Donalds but much sparsely populated country for which the northern and southern boundaries are taken as the B711 and B709 roads.

**TRANSPORT**
*Bus:* Carlisle to Lockerbie and Moffat; daily.
Lockerbie to Boreland and Sandyford; schooldays and Saturday.
Lockerbie to Langholm; Monday to Saturday.
Langholm to Eskdalemuir; Monday, Wednesday, Saturday and schooldays.
Glasgow to Moffat and Dumfries; daily.
Edinburgh to Moffat and Dumfries; Friday, Saturday and Sunday.
Edinburgh to Teviothead and Carlisle; daily.
Moffat to Bodesbeck; schooldays.
Hawick to Craik; Monday to Saturday.
Peebles to Gordon Arms and Galashiels; Monday to Friday.
Selkirk to Ettrick; schooldays.
Melrose to Moffat and St Mary's Loch; Tuesday and Thursday (July to September).

**ACCOMMODATION**
Hotels at Beattock, Moffat, Johnstone Bridge, Langholm, Eskdalemuir, St Mary's Loch, Ettrickbridge, Tushielaw, Buccleuch and Yarrow crossroads.
Camping at Beattock, Moffat, Ettrick Valley, St Mary's Loch.
Youth Hostels at Roberton (Snoot) and Broadmeadows. Bothy at Over Phawhope (182 082)

**MAPS**
Ordnance Survey 1:50,000, Sheets 78 and 79
Bartholomew 1:100,000, The Borders

of moderate height, trees can grow to the skylines - and often do! An extensive network of forest roads has been created, however, which can take walkers or cyclists far from the crowds and can facilitate through-routes being made.

An interesting feature of the Ettrick Hills concerns the valleys on either side of the ridge running seven kilometres from Herman Law to Bodesbeck Law. Moffat Water lies to the north-west of the ridge with Ettrick Water running parallel on the south-east side but flowing in the opposite direction. Birkhill at the head of the Moffat Water and Potburn near the head of the Ettrick Water are high starting points for the hills at approximately the same height. Birkhill is at the east end of Moffatdale though while Potburn is at the west end of the Ettrick Valley and the hills between are part of the watershed between the Atlantic Ocean and the North Sea.

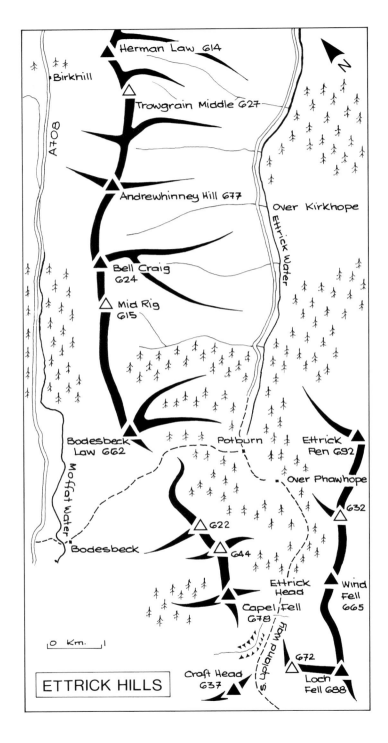

Herman Law 614
Birkhill
Trowgrain Middle 627
A708
Andrewhinney Hill 677
Over Kirkhope
Ettrick Water
Bell Craig 624
Mid Rig 615
Bodesbeck Law 662
Potburn
Ettrick Pen 692
Over Phawhope
Moffat Water
632
622
644
Bodesbeck
Ettrick Head
Wind Fell 665
Capel Fell 678
O Km. I
Ram Upland
S. Upland
672
Croft Head 637
Loch Fell 688

**ETTRICK HILLS**

# THE HILLS

**Herman Law** (614m)

The line of hills running south of the A708 towards Moffat starts here above the Birkhill Pass. This is the most northerly and easterly of the Ettrick Hills and also one of the easiest to climb because of the height of the road. It is as well to park at the Grey Mare's Tail car park and walk up the road, or the old grass-covered road alongside, to Birkhill as few walkers will want to climb Herman Law on its own.

Birkhill was once a toll house and has a plaque on its wall to Charles Lapworth, whose discovery of graptolites in this district led to the placing of the Silurian and Ordovician periods in their respective order in geological time. Lapworth's researches were mainly in Dob's Linn, one kilometre to the west.

A fence can be followed from Birkhill up the north side of the burn to Herman Law. The start is steep but quickly rewards the effort with a fine view over the pass to White Coomb. Three fences meet at the grassy summit, with the south fence leading over a boggy col to Trowgrain Middle. Layers of peat have been eroded from the col leaving a number of prominent and isolated tables of peat defying the elements under a thatch of heather and rough grasses.

**Andrewhinney Hill** (677m)

This hill can be climbed directly from the Grey Mare's Tail car park which lies beneath it. The ascent and descent are very steep but straightforward. The hill is more likely to be climbed in a ridge walk including Herman Law and Bell Craig.

Coming from Herman Law, a fence is followed over Trowgrain Middle (627m) and Mid Rig (650m) to the summit. Trowgrain Middle is a Donald top about two kilometres north-east of Andrewhinney Hill and has a tall squarish cairn of flat stones by the fence. The summit contour extends some distance north-west of the cairn with slightly rising ground requiring a slight diversion for the faithful collector of tops. Mid Rig sits midway between Trowgrain Middle and Andrewhinney Hill and has a well built stone man of thin flattish stones. The ridge follows a general south-westerly direction from Herman Law to Andrewhinney Hill and onward to Bell Craig, but the fence takes a zigzag course between these points to keep on the high ground. A cairn by the east-west facing fence marks the summit of Andrewhinney Hill. It is worth going down the slope at the western end of the fence until a great view opens out to the Grey Mare's Tail and Loch Skeen beyond.

**Bell Craig** (624m)

This hill lies about halfway between Herman Law and Bodesbeck Law and will be taken en route by most walkers in a complete traverse of this ridge. Those with less stamina can reach it from the Ettrick Valley leaving the public road about two kilometres from Potburn and following a road up Range Cleuch to the East Grain. The descent from Bell Craig to the Moffat Water is very steep and is hampered by conifers scattered across the slope.

*Bodesbeck Law from Capplegill*

The route back by Andrewhinney Hill is simpler and avoids the problem of crossing the Moffat Water. Mid Rig (615m) is a Donald top one kilometre south-west of Bell Craig. A fence leads from Bell Craig to Mid Rig and south-west over a rise (607m) to Bodesbeck Law.

### Bodesbeck Law (662m)
Although it is fairly centrally placed in the Ettrick range, Bodesbeck Law is rather distant from its neighbours. It sits at the west end of the chain which looks down on the Moffat Water, where the range turns south away from the valley towards Ettrick Head. A right of way crosses the range to the south of the hill from Bodesbeck on the Moffat Water to Potburn on the Ettrick Water, and offers a good approach from both directions.

The route from Potburn has a higher start and leaves the Ettrick Valley immediately to the south of the farm and follows a forest road north-west to the col. The fence and wall marking the regional boundary are followed north-west to the summit cairn. This is a good viewpoint for the big hills north of the Moffat Water.

If traversing the ridge from the Herman Law direction, the fence along this ridge joins up with a stone wall on the north ridge of Bodesbeck Law. A direct descent can be made from this hill to the A708, but it is hampered by steep ground, electric fences

*Craigmichan Scar and the Selcoth Burn from the slopes of Croft Head*

and ruined bridges over the Moffat Water. The less adventurous course is to return over Bell Craig to Andrewhinney Hill, or descend by the right of way to Bodesbeck.

## Capel Fell (678m)

This is a rather retiring hill in the group. It stands above Ettrick Head on the west, and is linked distantly to Bodesbeck Law and the northern chain of Ettricks by an irregular ridge of tops which drops to 480m at the pass between Potburn and Bodesbeck Farm. Ettrick Head to the south-east is a slightly higher pass, beyond which ridges rise south to Loch Fell, and east and north-east to Wind Fell and Ettrick Pen.

The grandest feature of Capel Fell is Craigmichan Scar where the southern slopes have been torn away above the Selcoth Burn. The scenery is quite savage on this side of the hill and is far-removed from the mild outlines normally associated with the Southern Uplands.

The easiest route to the hill is from the Ettrick Valley. A forest road can be followed from Potburn past Over Phawhope nearly to Ettrick Head. A path continues to the col where the fence can be followed north-west to the summit.

*Croft Head from the slopes of Loch Fell*

The start from the A708 crosses the Moffat Water by a bridge at Sailfoot and takes a track up the north bank of the Selcoth Burn. The track can be followed up the glen on the south-west side of Capel Fell or a way made up the slopes east of this to the ridge above Craigmichan Scar.

To see the Scar at close quarters, the Selcoth Burn can be crossed by a bridge opposite a sheep ree and the path followed along the northern slopes of Croft Head to the wind gap between Croft Head, Capel Fell and Loch Fell's north-west top. A rough descent can be made to the burn from there and its course followed by picking a way among the boulders.

The summit of Capel Fell is slightly north of the junction of three fences. A fence, then a wall follows the high ground north from the summit to the col to Bodesbeck Law passing over Smidhope Hill (643m) and White Shank (621m), which are both Donald tops, and another top (566m).

### Croft Head (637m)
The bridge over the Moffat Water at Sailfoot gives access to this hill which is somewhat isolated from the others in the range by intervening glens. Follow the

road to just north of Selcoth and take the vehicle track zigzagging up the slope on the north side of the Selcoth Burn. Once in the valley between a west top of Capel Fell and Croft Head, cross a bridge to the south side of the Selcoth Burn. The northern slopes of Croft Head are broken into steep scree scars and a path traverses airly above the burn to the col between Croft Head and Loch Fell. An east ridge leads steeply up to Croft Head from there, giving fine views of the gorge below. An easier but duller route to the hill passes Selcoth and climbs the north-west ridge to Croft Head.

The hill can also be climbed from a bridge over the Moffat Water two kilometres south-east of Moffat (107 043). This route follows the Southern Upland Way up the Cornal Burn past Craigbeck Hope on a forest road until it turns down the Wamphray Water. A firebreak by a burn leads north to the col east of Croft Head from where the east ridge can be ascended.

### Loch Fell (688m)
Loch Fell is the remotest of the Ettrick Donalds and is cloaked with forest to the east and west. It lies south of Ettrick Head and may be ascended best from that direction, following the forest road from Potburn and Over Phawhope in the Ettrick Valley up under Wind Fell. From the stile at Ettrick Head it is a simple task to climb south up the north ridge to Loch Fell. The hill can also be climbed from the A708 following the routes to Croft Head which is only two kilometres away to the north-west.

A long but simple route from the south-east starts from Garwaldwaterfoot, three kilometres north of Eskdalemuir. The private road on the south side of the Garwald Water is followed to Kiddamhill. This continues as a forest road over a shoulder of Dun Moss. The road reaches its highest point one kilometre south of Loch Fell with a fence leading directly from it to the summit where four fences cross beside a trig point. A return can be made over Cauld Law, continuing on a firebreak along the crest of its south-east ridge. Other firebreaks lead from this down to the nearby road going north of Thickside. From it, a road over the col west of Thickside rejoins the road to Kiddamhill.

The ridge and fence going north-west from Loch Fell dip then rise slightly before a deeper dip leads to a north-west top whose highest point lies south of the fence beyond a square of ditches. The view north from there can be very good.

A southern approach to the hill starts from the minor roads east of the A74 and River Annan between Beattock and Johnstonebridge. The road from Wamphraygate can be driven to Laverhay east of the Wamphray Water. The high vehicle track is taken from a gate, then a left fork above earthworks, dropping to cross a burn and follow the Wamphray Water past Kirkhill Cottage. The road climbs the west slopes of Ewelairs Hill to the col to its north, and a fence is followed above the forest over Cowan Hill to Loch Fell.

The return can be varied by dropping to a source of the Wamphray Water between the north top and Croft Head. The Southern Upland Way is followed southwards down the glen to a forest road where the Way should be left and the

*Looking towards Ettrick Pen from Over Phawhope*

road taken to the south towards the ruin at Garrogill. The Wamphray Water is followed to regain the outward route under Ewelairs Hill.

### Wind Fell (665m)

This is the easiest of the five Donalds to climb around Ettrick Head. The hill stands only three kilometres away from the end of the public road in the Ettrick Valley and a fairly sheltered walk follows the forest road past Potburn and Over Phawhope to the head of the valley. From the col at Ettrick Head it only requires a climb of 150m up the fence to the east over a distance of 800 metres to reach the summit, so it can be a good outing for a bad day.

### Ettrick Pen (692m)

This is the highest hill in the range and the only Donald on the south side of the Ettrick Valley except for Wind Fell at Ettrick Head. It can be reached easily from this valley by following the track from the road-end past Potburn to Over Phawhope. A bridge crosses the Ettrick Water here to the cottage and a broad firebreak leads east from it to grassy slopes leading to the summit. A ridge leads south-west to a top called Hopetoun Craig (632m) midway to Wind Fell. A double row of fence posts along this ridge makes an odd no man's land along the district boundary. Apart from this ridge, Ettrick Pen is almost surrounded by forest, but a longer route is possible from the east from the B709 at Glendearg following the Glendearg Burn.

*Loch of the Lowes and St Mary's Loch from Peat Hill*

## PATHS AND WALKS

*Craik to Eskdalemuir*. Encroaching conifers in Craik Forest tend to hide the line of a Roman road at sections between these two points, but the crossing can still be made and is facilitated by using neighbouring stretches of modern forest road. There is a car park and picnic site at Craik to start the route (348 080). A forest road goes north-west from the west end of this to join the line of the Roman road which runs to Craik Cross Hill (451m) which was a Roman Signal Station. The wide view from here to the Solway and Cheviots is threatened by the sprouting trees. The Roman road reaches its summit here in a V-shaped trench along a line between the Eildons and Criffel, and drops south-west along the edge of the forest to join a forest road beyond Lamblair Knowe which leads to Raeburnfoot and Eskdalemuir. (15 kilometres).

*Riskinhope to Scabcleuch*. This fine short walk gives a good view of the Loch of the Lowes as it leaves the south end of that loch at Chapelhope on the A708 and climbs west of Peat Hill to cross Pikestone Rig. East of Peniestone Knowe a junction post points the way down to the Ettrick Valley at Scabcleuch or Ettrickhill. The Southern Upland Way follows the route from Scabcleuch past Peniestone Knowe to Earl's Hill and St Mary's Loch. (6 kilometres).

# CHAPTER 10

# The Culter Hills

| | | |
|---|---|---|
| Culter Fell | 748m | 053 291 |
| Chapelgill Hill | 696m | 068 304 |
| Gathersnow Hill | 688m | 059 257 |
| Hillshaw Head | 652m | 048 246 |
| Hudderstone | 626m | 022 272 |
| Whitelaw Brae | 577m | 004 260 |

This range is separated from the Tweedsmuir Hills and Moffat Hills to the east by the River Tweed. The River Clyde rises to the west and flows north around the Culters forming a south-western, western and north-western boundary. The northern boundary to the range is formed by the Biggar Water and the Biggar Gap, through which the River Clyde escapes to the north-west. The plain between Biggar and Broughton is a watershed for the Southern Uplands between the Firth of Clyde and the North Sea, but the land is so level here that at time of flood some of the Biggar Water has found its way to the River Clyde while the main water has taken its normal course east to the River Tweed and the North Sea.

The Culter Hills (pronounced *Cooter* ) continue the line along the northern edge of the Southern Uplands handed on by the Broughton Heights, Moorfoots and Lammermuirs. Tinto Hill and the Pentlands are conspicuous variants from the line to the north. The Donalds in the Culter Hills are grouped in the north-east of the range. Four of them are linked in a U-shaped formation around the Culter Water-head Reservoir, while one of them is on an outlying ridge which extends the U to the east.

The Midlock Water, Camps Water and Wandel Burn are the main west-flowing streams. The Camps Water has been dammed to form the largest of four reservoirs in the area. The glen of the Culter Water forms an important gap in the range to the north and has been dammed to form the second largest reservoir in the area. The Culter Water is joined from the west by the Cow Gill which originates as the Duncan Gill in a deep glen running parallel to the Culter Water. The Cowgill Upper Reservoir is linked to the Cowgill Lower Reservoir by the Eastside Burn in this glen of many names.

## ACCESS
The A701 and A702 bound the range to the east and west respectively with the A702 giving way to the A73 and A74 in the west. The B7016 from Biggar to Broughton links the A702 to the A701 in the north, though several minor roads to the south of it come nearer the hills. A minor road south from Coulter penetrates well into the hills to the Culter Waterhead Reservoir, but local policy appears to have changed to discouraging private vehicles from passing a gate beyond Culter Allers Farm. The Cowgill Reservoirs road to the west is also reached from this point. Roads from Crawford in the west to Camps Reservoir and the Midlock Water run well into the range, but leave walkers a long way from the higher hills. In the east there is a private road into the Kingledoors Glen from north of Tweedsmuir and a very useful road up the Holms Water to Glenkirk from south of Broughton.

## TRANSPORT
*Bus:* Edinburgh to Coulter, Crawford and Dumfries; daily.
Biggar to Broughton and Peebles: Monday to Saturday.
Edinburgh to Moffat and Dumfries; Friday, Saturday and Sunday.

*Postbus:* Biggar to Tweedsmuir; Monday to Saturday.

## ACCOMMODATION
Hotels at Biggar, Broughton, Tweedsmuir, Crawford and Abington.
Camping at Wiston Lodge.
Youth Hostel at Wanlockhead.

## MAPS
Ordnance Survey 1:50,000, Sheet 72 for all the Donalds and Sheet 78
Bartholomew 1:100,000 The Borders. The western part of the range is not shown.

The glens of the Kilbucho Burn, Holms Water and Kingledoors Burn run to the north-east as tributaries of the River Tweed, and maintain the drier characteristic of the eastern side of the uplands by being without any loch or reservoir. The Kilbucho Glen has been glacially breached and shows little change of altitude over seven kilometres on the valley floor, though the road rises steeply along the side of the glen. As in the Biggar Gap, the watershed is so level in the Kilbucho Glen that floodwater may go east or west fairly well as it pleases. This is an area of numerous low, rounded hills and prehistoric and medieval sites ranging from hill forts and settlements to cultivation terraces, while a crannog occupied the valley floor before it became better drained.

The importance of the area for water supply to Strathclyde limits the freedom of the general public to wander at will. Access is not encouraged to the reservoir areas to prevent pollution, so walkers need to be resourceful, circumspect and considerate in exercising their freedom. The heathery hills are also tended for the annual fostering and dispatching of grouse, in which cycle hillwalkers are unwelcome.

A considerable area of hilly country which does not quite reach Donald height lies to the west and south of the main chain of the Culter Hills. Whitelaw Brae is the highest summit in this area and sits at the head of the forested Wandel Glen, around

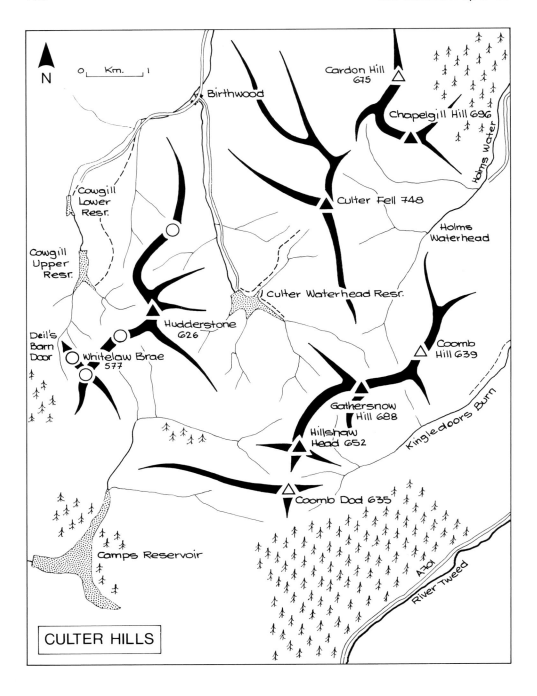

N

0    Km.    1

Birthwood

Cardon Hill
675

Chapelgill Hill 696

Holms Water

Cowgill
Lower
Resr.

Culter Fell 748

Holms
Waterhead

Cowgill
Upper
Resr.

Culter Waterhead Resr.

Hudderstone
626

Coomb
Hill 639

Deil's
Barn
Door

Whitelaw Brae
577

Kingledoors Burn

Gathersnow
Hill 688

Hillshaw
Head 652

Coomb Dod 635

A701

River Tweed

Camps Reservoir

CULTER HILLS

which a ridge runs from Whiteside Hill over Ewe Hill, Hardrig Head, Whitelaw Brae, The Seat and Rome Hill to Tewsgill Hill. The southern limb of this ridge faces south to the Camps Water and its reservoir and also forms part of a longer and more tortuous chain running around that valley over Whitelaw Brae, Hudderstone, Hillshaw Head, Culter Cleuch Shank, Whitecamp Brae, Risingclaw Heights and Yearngill Head. Yearngill Head, Black Dod, Clyde Law, Harleburn Head and Rodger Law in turn form a third U-shaped chain at the south of this area around the Midlock Water. Clyde Law sends down the Clydes Burn to the summit of the A74 and west coast mainline railway at Beattock on the watershed between the rivers Clyde and Annan (or firths of Clyde and Solway), but the highest source of the Clyde must be searched for in the Lowther Hills to the west.

The shortage of distinctive hills coupled with a mean summit level within the tree-planting limit, make this south-western zone of the Culters unattractive to many walkers. If, however, they are willing to brave the hazards of Midge Hill, Bog Hill, Mossy Dod and Snickert Knees, they will explore a large area of country which is seen by few and which has some rewarding views to offer both internally and externally.

## THE HILLS

### Culter Fell (748m)
This is the highest hill in the range. An old couplet puts it on a par with Tinto Hill to the north-west -

> "Between Tintock Top and Coulter Fell
> But scarce three handbreadths and an ell".

The couplet is inaccurate, for Culter Fell overtops Tinto by 41m, but it does show the importance of both hills in the area. They are easily recognised and are well known to road users, while few other hills here are known by name or sight to people outside the district.

Culter Fell is an easy hill to climb. A walk of one kilometre south from Culter Allers Farm on the Culter Water leads to the heathery north-west ridge which rises steadily to the summit. If a start is made over Knock Hill from Culter Waterhead farther up the glen, a rewarding view looks over the reservoir. Or the best of the view can be sacrificed for an easy road ascent farther on, climbing by the Lang Gill to the col east of Knock Hill, then on to the summit from the west.

The hill can also be reached from Glenkirk on the Holms Water. By following the track to Holms Waterhead, a route can be made up Leishfoot Hill to reach the summit from the south. Alternatively, a longer round can take in Chapelgill Hill from Glenkirk, or a start can be made over Congrie Hill and a ridge taken north-west to swing round to the summit from the north.

A trig point on a mound and a cairn mark the summit by a fence which runs along the main ridge in a north to south direction. The ridge drops to the south to a

*Culter Waterhead Reservoir from Knock Hill*

col, rises 30m over Moss Law, then drops again to Holm Nick, where a road comes up the Culter Water from its reservoir.

### Chapelgill Hill (696m)
This is another easy Donald to reach in the range. It stands only one and a half kilometres north-west of Glenkirk on the Holms Water and can be climbed from there in an ascent of some 420m. Its summit ridge continues over a rise in a curve to the north to Cardon Hill (675m), forming an east-facing corrie-like bowl which is quite distinctive as seen from the A701.

From the intermediate rise, a ridge goes south-west to Culter Fell and allows a round to be made with hills south of the Holms Water. Chapelgill Hill can also be climbed from the Culter Water road. A track up King's Beck can be taken to the slopes of Tippet Knowe and the main ridge joined south of King Bank Head.

### Gathersnow Hill (688m)
This hill stands at the head of the Culter Water to the south-east of Culter Waterhead Reservoir, and at the head of the Holms Water on the watershed with the Kingledoors Burn. It also faces the Kingledoors Burn not far from its head and provides the highest source for that burn. Its snow-holding powers are therefore important for three fairly large streams – one flowing to the Clyde and two to the Tweed.

The hill is usually climbed in a round of the Culter Waterhead Reservoir. If coming from Culter Fell a road is crossed at Holm Nick and a big climb taken up Glenwhappen Rig. If the northwards bulging rig did not exist, the source of the Culter Water would probably flow to the Tweed instead of the Clyde.

Gathersnow Hill can also be climbed from Glenkirk on the Holms Water. The ridge on the south side of the Holms Water can be followed from Glenlood Hill (566m). The going is soft on the ridge but is aided by a vehicle track west of the fence. A cairn is passed on Coomb Hill (639m) and easier grass slopes lead on to the main summit, while views can be enjoyed south to both Talla and Fruid reservoirs and north to Culter Waterhead Reservoir.

### Hillshaw Head (652m)
This hill sits to the south of the Culter Waterhead Reservoir and is rather awkward to reach. If taken in the round of the Donalds from Culter Fell over Gathersnow Hill, it is an extra burden on a distant ridge before the walker can turn northwards back to base over a long arduous piece of upland territory to Hudderstone. The ridge from Gathersnow Hill is grassy and straightforward enough with a fence for guidance, but the ridge extends another 800 metres beyond Hillshaw Head to Coomb Dod (635m), requiring the re-ascent of Hillshaw Head if all the tops are to be bagged on this round.

The hill can be taken on its own from the Tweed valley south of Tweedsmuir by those undaunted by forest. Leave the A701 at (054 203) and follow a forest road up Old Burn. Take a branch going north round the east side of Peddirie Dod and round the ridge of North Black Dod. This road continues round the east side of Ewe Hill, but leave it just after it crosses the Glenbreck Burn and follow the burn up for about 100 metres to take a firebreak north-east then another north-west. By contouring westwards along another, open slopes west of the forest can be reached leading to a 573m top. Continue north with a fence to Coomb Dod where a trig point sits on a knoll at the summit. The fence continues north across a 30m drop and up to Hillshaw Head, where a small cairn is tightly constrained within an enclosing fence.

The return can be made westwards from the 573m top by a fence to Culter Cleuch Shank and south over North Black Dod to Whitecamp Brae, but the going is arduous. From Whitecamp Brae descend north-east to a firebreak going down to rejoin the outward route.

### Hudderstone (626m)
This hill is shown as Heatherstane Law on older maps. It is easily reached from Culter Waterhead. The Culter Water is crossed by a bridge under the dam and the steep slopes climbed to Snowgill Hill from which there is a splendid view of the range over the reservoir. A walk of 600 metres leads to the summit of Hudderstone.

From Culter Allers Farm another route can follow the road for Cowgill past Birthwood and branch straight up the Cowgill Rig on a vehicle track. This gives a fine airy walk above the glens. A direct line to Hudderstone can be taken from a gate at the summit of the road, or the road can be followed steeply down to Cowgill Upper

*The Culter Hills seen across the River Tweed from Dulyard Brae*

Reservoir and Todlaw Rig ascended to Windgate Bank for a fine view over the reservoirs to Tinto Hill. The V-shaped cleft of the Windgate west of Hudderstone and the pink scree gash of the Deil's Barn Door beyond Duncan Gill are impressive.

A return to Birthwood can be made from Hudderstone along its north ridge over Woodycleuch Dod and Ward Law, or a descent made eastwards to the road at Culter Waterhead.

### Whitelaw Brae (577m)
A public road runs up the Camps Water to a junction about 800 metres west of the Camps Reservoir. The road uses the course of the railway line which was built for the construction of the dam, passing through the bank and ditch of an oval shaped henge monument east of the farm road to Normangill. Access to the reservoir is discouraged, so park west of the junction and follow a vehicle track north across two burns to Trow Hill. Contour between the hill and Cowhill, cross the burn and ascend the west ridge of Craig Hill (493m) for a fine view over the reservoir.

Continue north along the spongy ridge to Pinnacle (555m), which is an odd designation for a very ordinary rise, then follow the fence running eastwards to Ewe Hill. Keep with the fence as it turns north to Duncangill Head, where it splits north-west to Whitelaw Brae and north-east over a rise to Windgate Bank and Hudderstone.

*Looking from Glenlood Hill to Glenkirk and Culter Fell*

Whitelaw Brae has a trig point and gives a good view to the Cowgill Upper Reservoir from which it can also be reached (see Hudderstone). The ridge north-west of Whitelaw Brae leads to the Deil's Barn Door at the next col. This is a gap between a vegetated crag and an overhanging rock face at a steep and unstable source of the Wandel Burn running west to an extensive forest.

# CHAPTER 11

# Eaglesham and Dalmellington to Clydesdale

| | | |
|---|---|---|
| **Tinto** | 707m | 953 344 |
| **Cairn Table** | 593m | 724 243 |
| **Benbeoch** | 464m | 496 083 |
| **Loudoun Hill** | 316m | 608 379 |

**ACCESS**

The outside boundaries for this loose knit area run from East Kilbride by the B764 and A77 to Kilmarnock, A76 to Cumnock, B7046, B730 and A713 to Dalmellington, B741 and A76 to New Cumnock and Crawick, B740 to Crawfordjohn, A74 and A73 by Roberton to Lanark, and A72, A744 and A726 to East Kilbride. Loudoun Hill is reached from the A71 and Cairn Table from the A70.

**TRANSPORT**

*Bus:* Lanark to Thankerton, Symington and Biggar; daily.
Glasgow to Eaglesham; daily.
Hamilton to Strathaven and Galston; Monday to Saturday.
Kilmarnock to Darvel; daily.
Ayr to Cumnock and Cumnock to Muirkirk; Monday to Saturday.
Ayr to Dalmellington; daily.

**ACCOMMODATION**

Hotels at East Kilbride, Eaglesham, Kilmarnock, Cumnock, Symington, Wiston Lodge, Sanquhar, Strathaven, Biggar, Darvel, Fenwick, Sorn and New Cumnock.
Camping at Wiston Lodge and Cumnock.

**MAPS**

Ordnance Survey 1:50,000, Sheets 64, 71, 72 and 77

This chapter includes several very distinctive hills which are landmarks in their districts, but they are all isolated and do not combine to form a range. They all stand north of the Southern Uplands fault line so they have space to display themselves well in fairly low-lying areas where competition from other hills is either scarce or non-existent.

The area covered here forms the hinterland separating the old counties of Renfrew, Ayr, Lanark and Dumfries. As such it is an important lung for a sizable population who can find it useful for short outings and a few longer ones, though the A70 and A71 cut west to east across the region dividing it into thirds. The central section is further divided in half by the A723 running between Strathaven and Muirkirk.

Tinto, in the east, is the highest hill in the chapter. It is one of the best-known hills in the Southern Uplands and has the rare distinction of having good paths to its summit which generally allow walkers to keep their feet dry.

Cairn Table lies to the south of the A70 like Tinto, but is a considerable distance farther west and fails by about 15m to join it in Donald's Tables. It is the summit of a very extensive wilderness area which offers hard walking to those who like their own company.

Benbeoch and Loudoun Hill are close to roads and do not present much of a challenge in distance or height by their normal approaches. Both are very rocky little hills though, and the latter in particular offers some hard rock climbing.

More prosaic exercise can be had to the unimpressive Chair Stone on Distinkhorn (384m) south of Darvel, the ancient cairns on Blackside farther south, the Marriage Stone on Middlefield Law north of Muirkirk, or the Covenanting martyr sites at Auchingilloch (714 358) and Priesthill (730 315). Open-cast coal mining north of the A70 and B741 is limiting exploration. A five-minute walk north from a high point on the B764 to Ballageich Hill south-west of Eaglesham can reward with a splendid panorama of hills in the Highlands, Islands and Southern Uplands.

Corsencon Hill (475m) east of New Cumnock is another easily reached view-point, offering a fascinating view of the River Nith as it wriggles its way back into the Southern Uplands after having escaped. There are limestone workings at Craig-dullyeart to its north-west, with impressive caverns and flooded quarries.

Splendid river gorge scenery can be enjoyed on the River Clyde at New Lanark from (881 422), and on the River Ayr at Ballochmyle from (513 255). The linns at New Lanark are magnificent when the river is in flood, while the red vertical cliffs at Ballochmyle set off well the largest stone arch rail viaduct in Britain.

## THE HILLS

### Tinto (707m)

Tinto has a distinctive shape and is easily recognised from afar in its isolated situation. It can be picked out from some of the hills in the Southern Highlands as well as many in the Southern Uplands. As it is an easy hill to climb and is within reach of numerous towns, it is one of the most visited hills in the south of Scotland. The contrast between the green vegetation on the hill and the red felsite scars on its exposed flanks is very striking, while purple heather and dazzling snow add their seasonal attractions.

*Tinto from the south-east*

There are two popular routes to the hill. That from the north starts just off the A73 near Thankerton. The minor road to the south is taken past Fallburn to a car park at the first bend in this road. A good path starts from there and goes south-south-west through two gates past an ancient fort with several obvious concentric ditches and ramparts. Grass and heather slopes are ascended to Totherin Hill where the path passes west of a cairn to climb a spur east of Maurice's Cleuch. This is a very prominent gash revealing Tinto's red underwear when seen from the north-west. The path takes the western edge of the spur across the screes and joins a fence coming up from the cleuch leading to the summit.

A shorter but steeper route starts from Wiston on the B7055 south of the hill. Visitors are welcome to pass through the grounds of the YMCA National Training Centre at Wiston Lodge and may park in the drive before the lodge (report at the lodge as a courtesy).

The route to Tinto is signposted through the grounds and takes a line between the campsite and three shelter belts heading straight up the hill towards the conical Dimple. The steep heathery outcrops of the Pap Craig are turned on the east on a zigzag path which has many minor variations. A quick descent can be made on this face using the higher scree runs.

*Cairn Table from the Garpel Water at Tibbie Pagan's Bridge*

Tinto's summit carries a massive prehistoric cairn, a trig point and a view indicator, and is crossed by several fences with stiles. The situation and uncluttered sight-lines make it an unrivalled viewpoint for panoramas of southern Scotland. The view indicator lists Lochnagar and Skiddaw among the hills that can be seen from here while Ailsa Craig, Kintyre and Arran line the western horizon. With the possible exceptions of the Ettricks and the Cheviots, all the main ranges of the Southern Uplands can be seen in reasonable visibilty. It is worth carrying binoculars up on a good day to enjoy picking out features from the landscape, which can include power stations and industrial plants, TV masts and town steeples by the Clyde from Ayr to Glasgow. Foreground interest includes the upper Clyde and its railway line.

A ridge runs west from Tinto to Lochlyock Hill (529m) while another runs east to Scaut Hill (586m). There are scanty remains of a tower house below the latter near a small reservoir.

### Cairn Table (593m)
This is a popular walk from Muirkirk. Cars can be taken to Kames on the south side of the village where iron workers' cottages and the Institute survive as reminders of this area's former coal and iron industries. A rough road south from Kames leads past a memorial to John Loudoun Macadam, the pioneer road-maker, on the site of tar kilns which he worked in association with Lord Dundonald.

The track can be followed to the Garpel Water and the hill ascended from the west, or a more direct route taken from Kames past water-filled quarries, disused lades, cultivation rigs and industrial mounds and hollows to the north-west slopes.

The summit trig point is flanked by two massive ancient cairns. That to the west has been reshaped as a conical war memorial. The hill is a very good viewpoint and looks to Ailsa Craig, Arran, the Southern Highlands, the Culters and Galloway.

The southern slopes of the hill have been badly denuded of vegetation and runnelled by erosion - possibly by a combination of heather burning, motor cycles and flash floods. Those in need of more exercise can descend the southern slopes to the Grindstone Rig (where there are good examples of peat tables) and continue over Stony Hill (562m) to Wardlaw Hill (497m). An ancient cairn on this hill has been reshaped as a memorial to a war victim.

**Benbeoch** (464m)
This hill is a short excursion from the B741 north-east of Dalmellington, starting from the road to Benbain. This ascent from the south-east crosses a former wagonway and climbs to a very rocky slope under the summit, where a tall dry-stone wall weaves an oval route around a chaotic area of boulders. The wall has an overhanging coping facing outwards and is shown as a fox warren on Armstrong's map of 1775, though the wall is shown as encircling Benbeoch at that time.

The eastern face of Benbeoch falls from the summit in a rocky scarp and offers some rock-climbing.

**Loudoun Hill** (316m)
This remnant of a volcanic plug north of the A71 and east of Darvel offers a very short expedition to walkers, but can be a considerable challenge to rock-climbers. An easy grassy slope from the west leads to the summit where there is a trig point and a memorial to a Scots victory under Robert the Bruce over an English force in 1307 at the foot of the hill. The route of a former railway also passes below the hill but has lost its fine viaduct across the valley. This was demolished as dangerous after much hard toil.

## PATHS AND WALKS

*Douglas to Crawfordjohn.* From the crossroads at the Z-bend on the A70 in Douglas take the Springhill Road and climb east of Springhill Farm on a wide track to Pagie Hill - a good viewpoint. Follow the ridge south to the ancient cairn which is a prominent landmark on Auchensaugh Hill and descend by a path to cross the Black Burn at a bridge. Cross a dyke on Middle Muir where a power line crosses and follow another dyke or fence to Blairhill and Crawfordjohn. (8 kilometres).

*Fingland to Spango Bridge.* Near the junction of the A76 and B740 between Sanquhar and Kirkconnel, a minor road goes north-west from Crawick to Fingland. A right of way continues past Blackgannoch, becoming a grassy track climbing along the south side of the Spango Water valley. This track climbs over the north shoulder of Shiel Hill to a col on the north-east ridge. It then descends on the south side of The Dod, where there is a splendid view, to the Crawick Water at Spango Bridge on the B740. (7 kilometres).

*Eaglesham to Darvel.* A right of way runs over the now much forested moors between these two settlements. Cars can be taken to Carrot 5 kilometres south of Eaglesham. Take the unmetalled road going south-west at the junction, which goes through plantations and round the west side of Myres Hill under a compound of wind generators operated by the National Engineering Laboratory. The road splits beyond Myres, with one branch going to the hilltop compound. Carry on along the lower route to the Birk Burn. Beyond this a spongy moor is crossed following marker posts south-east along the high ground of Crook Hill until a forest fence is reached. Descend south-west along the fence to a gate near the col. The Darvel TV transmitter mast can be used as a route marker from here. Follow a firebreak from the gate with occasional signs to help, curving south then south-west over a rise to a gate at High Overmuir and the track south to Darvel. (17 kilometres).

*Muirkirk to Glentaggart.* A path goes south-east from Muirkirk over the col between Cairn Table and Little Cairn Table. A firebreak leads through the forest on the east side of the Duneaton Water and joins a road after 500 metres. Beyond North Bottom, this road should be left where it crosses the Duneaton Water, and the stream followed east to the junction of the Auchandaff and Shawhead roads. A public road leads on to Glentaggart and a bus route at Glespin. (20 kilometres).

*Muirkirk to Kirkconnel.* From Kames on the south side of Muirkirk, the old road is taken south up the Garpel Water past Cairn Table to cross the col between Wardlaw Hill and Stony Hill. The route heads south-east through the forest below Pepper Hill and Drummond Knowe to the Friarminnan Burn then goes south to Fingland where it becomes a tarred road. This is left at a bend to the east of Kirkland Hill and a col is crossed south-westwards to descend to Kirkland and Kirkconnel. (21 kilometres).

# CHAPTER 12

# Ardrossan to Greenock

| | | |
|---|---|---|
| **Hill of Stake** | 522m | 273 630 |
| **Kaim Hill** | 387m | 228 534 |

About 65 kilometres north of the Southern Uplands fault line, the districts of Renfrew, Inverclyde and Cunninghame meet in an area of upland moors and wide horizons. The summits here are sometimes known as the Renfrewshire Heights or the North Ayrshire Hills depending on the direction of approach. The area featured in this chapter is roughly triangular in shape. It is bounded to the north and west by the Firth of Clyde, and to the south-east by the Dalry to Johnstone Gap. Sitting on the south side of the Clyde estuary it is technically part of the Central Lowlands of Scotland. Although it does not contain any Donalds it rises to over 500m at several points and is undoubtedly upland in character to confound those who over-simplify Scotland's topography.

Equivalent in latitude to the Pentlands as northern outposts of the Southern Uplands, these hills are farther north than Arran and nearly as far north as the Paps of Jura and the hills of Cowal. The character of the hills south of the River Clyde is firmly allied to that of the Southern Uplands though, with coarse moorland grasses and heather underfoot and a scarcity of distinctive landmark forms over much of the area. Heavy going on the higher moors can be very tiring, particularly in wet seasons.

The rewards for tramping the zone are mainly in the views to the outside world. With the ground falling away to the Clyde and Central Lowlands, some of the views to be had to Arran, Cowal, the Arrochar Alps and over the coastlines are outstanding. Sedentary motorists enjoy renowned views over the Clyde estuary from above Gourock, Greenock and Port Glasgow without leaving their cars, and all along the coastline there are splendid views to be had, which are greatly enhanced by every gain of height. It is well worthwhile scaling the terraced heights above Largs at numerous points or the ringed fort on Knock Hill north of the town for the views of the Clyde and its islands.

Farther inland the views are more restricted but can be replaced by fine valley scenery as in Glen Garnock, the Calder Glen, and the glen of the Gogo Water leading back from Largs towards Irish Law. Near Dalry at Cleeves Cove (317 475) there is an impressive underground cavern on the Dusk Water.

**ACCESS**
The main approach from the east is by the M8 Glasgow-Greenock motorway and A737 Paisley-Kilwinning road. The A78 from Greenock to Irvine gives access to the western edge of the zone. The B786 and B788 Lochwinnoch to Port Glasgow and A760 Lochwinnoch to Largs roads are closer boundaries to the higher ground in the north along with a minor road along the Noddsdale Water from Largs to Greenock, which crosses amidst the numerous reservoirs in the north.

Just north of Lochwinnoch, from the B786, a side road climbs Glen Calder to the Muirshiel Country Park. Glengarnock, a parallel glen to the south, can be reached from minor roads north of Kilbirnie. The Gogo Glen east of Largs provides routes into the hills from the west. Twisting hill roads from Inverkip and from near IBM on the southern outskirts of Greenock lead to Loch Thom and the inland Largs to Greenock minor road. A steep but very scenic minor road climbs from Hunterston to Dalry.

**TRANSPORT**
Frequent public transport can be found around the margins of this region, bringing the hill country within reach of those without cars and adding particular benefit to lineal through-routes.

*Bus:* Glasgow to Greenock, Inverkip, Largs, Ardrossan and Irvine; daily.
Glasgow to Paisley, Johnstone and Kilbarchan; daily.
Johnstone to Lochwinnoch, Kilbirnie and Largs; daily.

*Trains:* Kilwinning and Paisley Gilmour Street are junction stations on the Glasgow to Stranraer line with services to Largs, and Wemyss Bay and Gourock. Frequent services operate daily. A Glasgow to Paisley Canal service runs from Monday to Saturday.

*Ferry:* Ardrossan to Brodick; Largs to Great Cumbrae; Wemyss Bay to Rothesay; and Gourock to Dunoon; all daily. A summer service from Gourock plies to Kilcreggan and Helensburgh.

**ACCOMMODATION**
Hotels at Ardrossan, Seamill, Largs, Skelmorlie, Wemyss Bay, Inverkip, Gourock, Greenock, Port Glasgow, Howwood, Johnstone and Dalry.
Camping at Barnbrock on the B786.

**MAPS**
Ordnance Survey, 1:50,000, Sheet 63

The volcanic rocks which form this hill region are generally well hidden under an accumulation of peat and coarse vegetation, but glaciation has played its part in shaping the landscape. Ice flowing from the Highlands has scoured across the area leaving arrays of crag and tail formations amidst the lava flows and creating problems for road engineers, particularly north of Lochwinnoch. The Clochodrick Stone (374 613) sitting by a road junction near Howwood is a massive glacial erratic laid down by the melting ice sheets. It is even big enough to provide some fun for those who enjoy rock scrambling.

The heart of the district is more of a tableland than a range of hills. Streams flow out from this zone in all directions, but the greater water courses such as the Rivers

Garnock, Calder and Gryfe escape inland to the east. The shorter streams flowing to the west generally have a steeper descent from the scarp-like slopes facing the Clyde, save for the longer Noddsdale Water which takes an easier south-west course to the sea at Largs. The impounding of streams for reservoirs to supply the needs of the towns around the fringes of the region has added foreground variety enhancing the views from the area. The ingenuity of the earliest schemes has created several notable walks which can be enjoyed for their historical interest as well as for their scenery.

The area has acquired an unhappy reputation as a graveyard for aircraft. Numerous planes have been wrecked in it as they sought to navigate past the misty hills to and from the airfields of the Central Lowlands, but modern navigational aids have eased the problem.

The Clyde-Muirshiel Regional Park has been designated over parts of the northern sector of the region. Lunderston Bay at Inverkip caters for those wishing to relax by the sea. The Castle Semple Water Park at Lochwinnoch provides facilities for water sports. There are visitor centres in more upland settings at Cornalees Bridge near Loch Thom and at the Muirshiel Country Park in Glen Calder above Lochwinnoch. There is an RSPB nature reserve at the south end of Castle Semple Loch.

Despite promises made in the early 1970s, the regional park has failed to provide official cross-country routes of serious length for walkers. Wherever possible walkers should co-operate with the park authorities and landowners, but few will feel constrained by the regulations to restrict their exercises to the few short nature trails provided.

## THE HILLS

### Hill of Stake (522m)
The highest part of this upland zone is Hill of Stake. It shows up from low ground to the north-east or from the Calder Glen, but from other directions it tends to be hidden and more of a moorland eminence of little distinction save for its height.

The Calder Glen provides a fairly short and easy route to the hill from the car park at the Muirshiel Country Park, by following a vehicle track to a disused barytes mine two kilometres north-east of the summit. The track looks back to an area of crag and tail hillocks beyond Windy Hill and its nature trail. Among these, Craig Minnan was reputed to be a conventicle site for Covenanters. Farther north on Duchal Moor there is a disused narrow-gauge railway track constructed in the 19th century for grouse-shooting parties. Laverock Stone (295 691) is an erratic boulder of no great size though it is significant for this bleak area.

Starting from Blackburn, two kilometres north of Kilbirnie, Glen Garnock provides a longer but finer approach to the hill. The track from Blackburn passes to the east of Glengarnock Castle, a ruinous tower house perched dramatically on a steep promontory over the river. The glen is very scenic opposite Murchan Hill. Here the Spout of Garnock plunges over a vertical drop in a narrow white plume as the glen ends in several gullies. The scenery above the falls changes completely and the heavy, tedious upland moors cannot be avoided.

A trig point crowns the summit of Hill of Stake at the junction of three electric fences, but these can be crossed fairly easily. The views extend to Islay, Jura, Fife and the Lothians and from Galloway to the Highlands. A little lochan south of the summit is a useful landmark for those passing east of it to drop to Glengarnock. The wreckage of a crashed aircraft lies in a hollow between the lochan and Hill of Stake.

For little extra climbing, the return can be made over two tops to the south-east, East Girt Hill and Misty Law. The latter is the most shapely and best known of the high tops in this area. A return can be made from it to Muirshiel Country Park for those starting from the Calder Glen by dropping down the north-east shoulder and fording the river.

Hill of Stake can be climbed from Largs by following Gateside Street and Flatt Street eastwards from the town centre past Largs Academy to Flatt Farm. Here a vehicle track climbs steeply to follow a shelf across the northern slopes of the Gogo Water's glen before the track drops to cross Greeto Bridge in the valley to the north.

A fairly direct route can be taken from the bridge contouring the southern slopes of the Greeto Water to Hill of Stake, or a longer approach can follow the west edge of the high ground on the other side of the valley for the views to the outside world. The trig point on Hill of Stake is a welcome landmark on the bleak upper stretches of this route.

A worthwhile expedition can be made over Hill of Stake between the railway stations at Largs and Glengarnock in about six hours.

**Kaim Hill** (387m)
This minor elevation comes well down the league of moorland heights in this section, but is unrivalled as a viewpoint in a district noted for superb views. It can be climbed easily from the Southannan to Dalry road which rises to 230m on the south side of the hill. Most people will wish to make a longer day of it starting at sea-level on the A78 and taking in Kaim Hill in passing as they cross over other heights in the area, such as Blaeloch Hill (406m), to reach the A760 or other return route.

A route from Fairlie Station takes a path up Fairlie Glen past Fairlie Castle and waterfalls to reach the northern slopes of the hill, and it can be continued through to Knockendon Reservoir and Dalry Station.

The best views from Kaim Hill are on the western slopes before the trig point summit is reached. The industrial developments below do not enhance the beauty of the scene, but they are impressive examples of human technology and endeavour, even if the planning was flawed. The deep-water terminal which was used by massive ore carriers exploited the trench dug to the east of the Cumbraes by Highland glaciers flowing south.

*Loch Thom*

Kaim Hill shows outcrops of millstone grit and was an industrial site itself long before Hunterston and Southannan were developed with nuclear power stations, ore stocking yards and an oil rig construction site. The millstone quarry is an interesting site and occupies a long ramp of Black Hill to the south-west of Kaim Hill. Sections of mill-stones can still be found around there.

## PATHS AND WALKS

*The Greenock Cut.* In 1827 an ingenious aqueduct designed by Robert Thom was opened to bring water from the Renfrewshire hills to the rapidly expanding town of Greenock. Loch Thom, named after this pioneer, is the largest of the reservoirs in the catchment area today. The now disused Greenock Cut follows a contour line running roughly westwards, then north and eastwards around Dunrod Hill (298m) and neighbouring hillocks to the slopes above Greenock. A pipeline through the hills from Loch Thom now bypasses the Cut, much reducing the flow of water in it.

The Cut can be joined at the Cornalees Bridge Visitor Centre at the west end of Loch Thom's compensation reservoir. A walkway follows the outside edge of the Cut and gives superb views over the Clyde to Bute, Cowal and the Arrochar Alps. At Overton, above Greenock, a vehicle track can be taken south-west to return to Loch Thom and Cornalees Bridge.

*The Kelly Cut.* The Kelly Burn separates the districts of Inverclyde and Cunning-hame in a succession of cataracts and enters the sea just to the south of Wemyss Bay Station. By following a road up the north bank for 150 metres, the start of a broad track will be found which climbs with the burn to an iron bridge. A narrower and more demanding path is taken, still on the north bank, or the water board road running nearby is joined to the Kelly Reservoir.

The Kelly Cut, constructed in the mid 19th century, diverted water north from this area and can be followed on its west bank as it contours Leap Moor to the compensation reservoir at Loch Thom. Walkers may continue towards Greenock along the Greenock Cut or take the road to Inverkip Station and the A78 from Cornalees Bridge. Inverkip may also be reached from a road which runs through Leapmoor Forest.to the west of the Kelly Cut.

*Ardrossan to Paisley.* A cycle-walkway joins these two points starting from the ferry terminal in Ardrossan. The route passes through the town centre and follows the promenade to Saltcoats and Stevenston dodging summer trippers or winter waves. Going inland over the level-crossing at Stevenston, it passes through Ardeer Park and follows minor roads to Kilwinning where it joins a cycle-walkway from Irvine.

The River Garnock is crossed by a tall viaduct on the north side of the town and a minor road followed east of Blair and Dalry and past Highfield and Davidshill to Longbar and Glengarnock, where it joins a disused railway past Kilbirnie and the north sides of Kilbirnie Loch and Barr Loch to Lochwinnoch. Water sculptures enliven the scenery in a cutting between the two lochs. The railway bed leads on to Johnstone and Paisley Canal with a short diversion along the main road at Elderslie between them.

*Johnstone to Greenock.* At a junction on the last route north of Johnstone, another former rail route has been converted to a cycle-walkway heading north-westwards through Houston and Crosslee to Greenock. The route crosses the River Gryfe by a fine viaduct at Bridge of Weir and counts off the miles to Kilmacolm with an entertaining series of wayside sculptures.

# CHAPTER 13

# The Lowther Hills

| | | |
|---|---|---|
| Lowther Hill | 725m | 890 107 |
| East Mount Lowther | 631m | 878 100 |
| Steygail | 573m | 888 084 |
| Green Lowther | 732m | 900 120 |
| Dun Law | 677m | 917 136 |
| Louise Wood Law | 618m | 932 153 |
| Well Hill | 606m | 914 065 |
| Comb Law | 645m | 944 075 |
| Ballencleuch Law | 689m | 936 050 |
| Scawd Law | 663m | 923 035 |
| Wedder Law | 672m | 939 025 |
| Gana Hill | 668m | 954 011 |
| Earncraig Hill | 611m | 973 014 |
| Queensberry | 697m | 989 997 |
| Auchenleck Hill | 447m | 921 990 |

Man-made additions to the summits of Green Lowther and Lowther Hill make this range conspicuous to travellers following the main road and rail routes between the west Central Lowlands and the English border. These routes follow the Nith valley on the west and the Annandale-Clydesdale gap on the east which form the main boundaries to the range. The Crawick and Duneaton waters form a north-west boundary which is also marked by the B740 road running between Crawick and Crawfordjohn.

The southern edge of the range merges with extensive forests and low ground in a wedge towards Dumfries between the Nith Valley and the A701 from Dumfries to Beattock. The minor road from Ae Bridgend on the A701 to Ae Village and its north-eastern continuation at a branch near Loch Ettrick are the effective boundaries in the south and west. There are numerous forest roads and ancient monuments south and east of Loch Ettrick, but most walkers will prefer the open slopes farther north. The Forest of Ae dates from 1927 and has several forest walks north of Ae Village, but suffers from the usual predominance of spruce. Ae was the first forest village in Scotland. Crichope Linn (914 953) near Thornhill is a spectacular chasm which is worth visiting by a path on the north side of the glen.

**ACCESS**

The B797 Mennock Pass and A702 Dalveen Pass roads, and the B7040 continuing from the former between Leadhills and Elvanfoot, bring all the hills of the northern and higher sector of the Lowthers within easy reach. The southern sector is best reached from minor roads approaching from the north and south. An access road from the A702 can be driven to the south end of the Daer Reservoir where a number of hills beckon. The same summits can be trodden from the south by taking minor hill roads east from Thornhill on the A76 which connect with Ae Village and the A701. Durisdeer, east of the A702, also gives access to this group from the west. Queensberry, at the south-east end of the range, can be visited from the south or from the Kinnel Water by a road from the A74 at Beattock to Kinnelhead.

**TRANSPORT**

*Bus:* Edinburgh to Abington, Crawford, Thornhill and Dumfries; daily.
Edinburgh to Beattock and Dumfries; Friday, Saturday and Sunday.
Glasgow to Beattock and Dumfries; daily.
Sanquhar to Wanlockhead and Leadhills; Monday to Saturday.
Ayr or Kilmarnock to Cumnock, Sanquhar and Dumfries; daily.
Dumfries to Ae Village; Monday to Saturday.

**ACCOMMODATION**

Hotels at Wanlockhead, Crawford, Beattock, Moffat, Sanquhar, Abington, Thornhill and Auldgirth.
Youth hostel at Wanlockhead. Bothies at Brattleburn (016 069) and Burleywhag (972 001).

Camping at Crawford, Moffat, Beattock, Closeburn and Sanquhar.

**MAPS**

Ordnance Survey 1:50,000, Sheet 78

The Mennock Pass and Dalveen Pass are very impressive glens dividing the range in north-east to south-west cuts at right angles to the A76 and A74 roads. The Mennock Pass carries the B797 to 468m between Wanlockhead and Leadhills. These are two of the highest villages in the country, with the former claiming the title for Scotland. The road splits at Leadhills with branches going north and east to the A74 at Abington and Elvanfoot. The Dalveen Pass is the lower and more southerly of the two passes with a summit on the A702 at 337m, but the hills rising steeply on both sides make it just as impressive. There is a small burial ground at the watershed on the A702 for the Lairds of Troloss. There are no villages along the A702 until Carronbridge and Elvanfoot are reached at either end, but the hamlet of Durisdeer lies just off to the east and is a good base for the hills to the east.

Leadhills and Wanlockhead are sizeable communities which have developed over centuries in connection with the exploitation of the mineral resources in the area. Deposits of gold, silver, lead and other minerals have been worked intermittently over the years and are still sought after from time to time by hopeful prospectors. The industrial archaeology of the area is well worthy of study and the mining museum at Wanlockhead and the Miners' Library of Leadhills should not be missed by those seeking an understanding of the area's heritage. Apart from workings between Wanlockhead and Leadhills, the main centres of industry were

*The summit of Lowther Hill*

down the Wanlock Water and Glengonnar Water. An ancient beam engine for pumping water from the mines can be seen on the east side of Wanlockhead near the Wanlock Water. Loch Nell mine in the same area is open to visitors.

The Daer Reservoir to the east of the Dalveen Pass is one of the largest sheets of water in the Southern Uplands and is only rivalled by St Mary's Loch between Galloway and the North Sea. The scheme was opened in 1956 to serve Lanarkshire.

## THE HILLS

### Lowther Hill (725m)
This is an easy climb from Wanlockhead since half the height above sea-level has already been conquered in reaching the village. An access road from the north end of the village leaves the B797 for the summit to fulfil the outing's designation as a stroll. A route from the south end of the village, used by the Southern Upland Way, passes a cemetery and contours south-west of Stake Hill to join this road higher up. The reddish-pink Lanarkshire chips used on this road contrast brightly with the green hillside. Wanlockhead has two cemeteries within the village, while the unhallowed summit of Lowther Hill was once used as a disposal point for suicide cases.

Summit baggers have a problem on Lowther Hill, as a radar station with two huge golf ball-like domes, red-brick buildings and pylons with dish aerials, all

*Green Lowther*

within a fenced compound, crown the hill masking the highest point. This appears to be a small rise just inside the fence on the south-east side.

The Southern Upland Way follows the regional boundary fence south-east over Cold Moss (628m) and Laght Hill (507m) to Over Fingland on the A702. A circular route can be made from there to Lowther Hill with the return over Green Lowther and one of its ridges. The view to the Dalveen Pass from Comb Head between Cold Moss and Laght Hill is one of the best in the range.

**East Mount Lowther** (631m)
With Green Lowther and Lowther Hill to its east, this hill is oddly named. It is the most westerly of the Donalds in the Lowther range and can be easily climbed along with the two mentioned. It is joined to Lowther Hill by a north-east ridge which drops 130m to a col at the summit of the Enterkin Pass.

The shortest route to East Mount Lowther is a steep and heathery climb from the B797 in the Mennock Pass. A more gradual graded route starts from Wanlockhead near the eastern cemetery and uses the Enterkin Pass track to the col at the foot of the north-east ridge. A longer and more satisfying route to this col is from the southern end of the pass (see paths and walks) returning over East Mount Lowther and Thirstane Hill (583m), or by a prominent little spur north-east of this hill which descends to the Enterkin Burn.

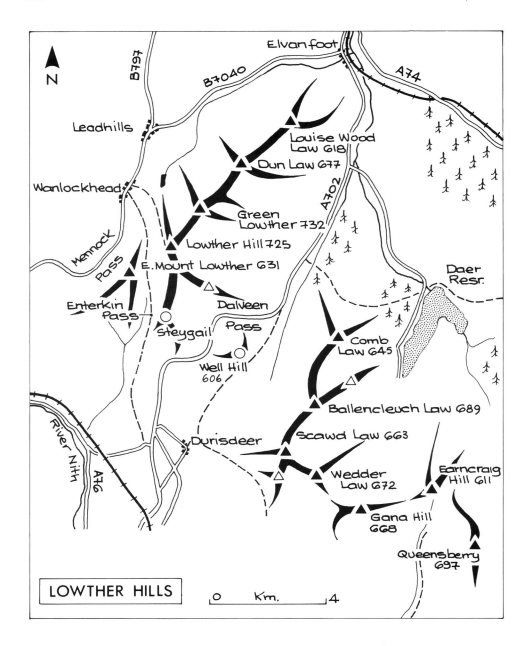

**Steygail** (573m)

This hill acts as a very bold view-stopper to those descending the Enterkin Pass to the south. As a result, it itself is the finest viewpoint for looking into the Enterkin Pass, though the northerly view will be spoiled by flat lighting conditions if a walker arrives at the top in the middle of the day. The hill is best climbed from the Lavern

Burn Bridge on the A702 where there is a parking area. A descent in a north-westerly direction to cross the Dalveen Lane leads to a gate through an electric fence and access to the south-east ridge of the hill. A return from the summit can be made over the rocky Dern Craig at the south end of this ridge for a good view of the Dalveen Pass.

### Green Lowther (732m)

The road to the summit of Lowther Hill continues north-east over an intervening rise to Green Lowther, providing the easiest route to the latter. If the huge white balls on Lowther Hill were teed up for a golfing giant, then Green Lowther would provide the natural green to aim at. The target flag is replaced however by a battery of dish aerials on a complex construction of uprights within a compound. The summit with its trig point is outside the compound and easily found.

A fence leads down the north-east ridge as a guide to those continuing to Dun Law. Peden Head, some 600 metres along this ridge is the turn-off point for those descending by Riccart Law Rig to the A702. The Riccart Cleuch and Lang Cleuch offer more sheltered descent routes in foul weather once the steep drop from Green Lowther has been made. Both routes can come onto a track to Over Fingland. The deep bowl at the head of the Lang Cleuch and the smooth rounded spurs in this area exemplify the scenery of the Lowthers.

### Dun Law (677m)

A col at 570m separates this hill from Green Lowther's north-east ridge. If walking out to Dun Law, and perhaps Louise Wood Law beyond, and a return has to be made to Wanlockhead, then a decision has to be taken to either descend to the B7040 and walk up the road or else retrace steps along the ridge, with all the tiring up and down work involved. A compromise route contouring the slopes to the reservoir north-east of Green Lowther is interesting, but is not advised due to the steeply-gullied heathery slopes. The summit of the hill is slightly east of a fence and can of course be reached on its own easily from the B7040 near Hass or over Glen Ea's Hill, or from the A702 by the Glenochar Burn. The north side of Glen Ea's Hill shows scars where water was 'hushed' to expose the bedrock in mineral-working days.

### Louise Wood Law (618m)

This is another oddly named hill in the Lowthers and is shown as Lousie Wood Law on some older maps and in Donald's Tables. It is the most northerly Donald in the range and is easily climbed from the east, starting from the A702 near Elvanfoot. A Roman Road is crossed above the A702 if the ascent is made to the east ridge of Watchman Hill. As the name suggests, this is a good viewpoint at a crossing of valleys. The River Clyde, the A74 and the main Glasgow-Carlisle railway all lie below. A ridge climbs south and west from there to the trig point on Louise Wood Law. If continuing by the south-west ridge to Dun Law, there is a steep descent to a col at 500m under White Law. Louise Wood Law, Dun Law, and Green Lowther can be combined in a round from the A702 quite comfortably. The grain of the country makes a round of the three from the B7040 a bit more awkward.

**Well Hill** (606m)

This is the culmination of a piece of high ground which lies between the Dalveen Pass and the Well Pass. The latter runs north-east from Durisdeer along the south and east side of the hill and offers a good route to its southern slopes. Once at the summit the walker has a choice of routes to follow along twisting ridges to several other eminences to the north, west, and south-west. The ridges are worth visiting for the views of the passes, but some back-tracking is necessary to reach every vantage point.

*Well Hill above Dalveen Toll Cottage*

**Comb Law** (645m)
This hill sits between the A702 and Daer Reservoir. It can be climbed from the first by following the Well Path south towards the Kirkstane Grain to gain the western slopes of the hill. The route westwards from Daer Reservoir crosses the Kirkhope Cleuch and ascends the grassy eastern slopes. The hill is usually climbed with others to the south.

**Ballencleuch Law** (689m)
If approaching from Daer Reservoir, the best route to this hill goes south-west up Watchman's Brae and over Rodger Law (688m) where there is a trig point. If approaching from the A702, the Well Path can be followed until opposite the hill, or a visit can be made first to Comb Law and the rough ridge taken southwards with a fence over Hirstane Rig. The easiest route from Durisdeer goes up Durisdeer Rig on a vehicle track to a wall on Durisdeer Hill. The wall continues south-east along the high ground until the south-west ridge leads to Ballencleuch Law.

**Scaw'd Law** (663m)
This hill lies to the east of Durisdeer and can be climbed like the last one from the vehicle track which runs up Durisdeer Rig. A wall leads from Durisdeer Hill to Scaw'd Law. Alternatively, the road from the south end of Durisdeer can be taken past the cemetery and a track taken up the Blackgrain Shoulder. A south ridge runs out from Scaw'd Law to Glenleith Fell (611m) where a vehicle track south-west of the top leads back to the valley.

**Wedder Law** (672m)
This hill sits south-east of the last one and can be climbed with it from Durisdeer. The Glenaggart road leads south-east from Durisdeer past the cemetery and sends off a branch which climbs up the Tansley Rig to near the summit. This is higher than the 666m height shown on the map and given in Donald's Tables, otherwise Shiel Dod (668m) to the north-east would be the main summit. The 666m height is only a confusing spot height and is not the summit, so Wedder Law retains its status. The ridge over Ewe Gair and Shiel Dod is the recognised route to the hill from the south end of the Daer Reservoir.

**Gana Hill** (668m)
This hill can be climbed from Daer Reservoir to its north by following the track to Thick Cleuch and the north ridge of the hill, or by starting from Mitchellslacks in the south and following the track to Burleywhag and the south-east slopes. A small pile of stones marks the summit just north of a fence which runs west towards Wedder Law and east to Earncraig Hill. The prominent spur of Garroch Fell to the south-west may appear higher but is not. The Five Wells shown on the map to the west are green, mossy water holes. The streams on this side of the range are headwaters for the River Clyde.

**Earncraig Hill** (611m)
Like the last one, this hill can be reached from the Daer Reservoir by following the track to Thick Cleuch and climbing to Daer Hass, or by starting from Mitchellslacks

*The Daer Water at Watermeetings*

in the south and taking the track past Burleywhag to the same col. A steep ascent by a wall leads to the summit. James Hogg, The Ettrick Shepherd, stayed at Mitchell-slacks for a time. If returning to the Daer Reservoir, the long north ridge of Earncraig Hill can be followed over Lamb Hill and the Daer Water crossed at Crookburn. If continuing to Queensberry, the direct route across the V-shaped glen is steep and stony, while the diversion north-east along the fence around the higher ground is time-consuming and passes through peat hags and peat tables. There is a rocky crag on the east face of the hill on the line to Penbreck.

**Queensberry** (697m)
Because of its position on the southern edge of the Lowthers, Queensberry is a well-known landmark. It shows a graceful saddle shape to the west and appears as a cone from other directions. It is remote from major roads but can be reached from a number of directions.

From Mitchellslacks on the Thornhill to Ae Village road a track goes up the Capel Burn under The Law and past an ancient cairn. Where it crosses a terrace towards New House, leave it and take the grassy slopes leading directly to the large cairn on Queensberry.

A more interesting but longer route follows the track going east of The Law and strikes east for High Church (405m). To the south-south-west of this top there is a remarkable gully below a V-shaped rocky nick. Below the nick, the gully slants down between steep boulder-strewn slopes and an impressive buttress to flatten out at a small lochan. Continue to Wee Queensberry up its south-west ridge, with glacial drift scars breaking through the vegetation and boulder colonies and up-ended stones giving a rugged aspect not typical of the Lowthers.

The vast Forest of Ae lies closely to the east and south with the Ae Water's valley pointing to Criffel on the Solway. Wee Queensberry (512m) has a very distinctive summit ridge in the shape of a crag and tail. The summit rises steeply from the west to a trig point and a lower rounded rise to the east which falls away more gradually. A col to the north leads to Queensberry.

Although Queensberry appears as a uniformly grassy hill from a distance, it has a fair scattering of boulders on its upper slopes. Many of these boulders are pitted and pot-holed with erosion.

The hill can also be reached from Kinnelhead west of Beattock by walking along a private road to Lochanhead. Stay north of the field walls and join a fence north of the forest for a direct route to the summit. This is a dull but quick approach past several cairns and the Pot of Ae, a bowl-shaped depression which gathers the headwaters of the Water of Ae at the corner of the forest. A return from Queensberry can be made in this direction over Harestanes Heights and Craighoar Hill, which shows a craggy face to the Threepen Burn.

**Auchenleck Hill** (447m)
A vehicle track runs south-east from Durisdeer over the cols separating Nether Hill, Little Fell and Auchenleck Hill from the higher Lowthers to the north-east, and reaches the Thornhill to Ae Village road at Garroch Bridge (942 977) while a branch heads south-west beyond Nether Hill to Burn. The tracks, for shooting, can be of advantage to walkers seeking access to this side of the range, or seeking low-level walks on bad days. The circuit of Auchenleck Hill from Garroch Bridge is a fine walk, following the track under The Dod (422m) to the Berry Grain. After this is crossed, a footpath from Daerhead is joined following the north side of the White Snout to the Cample Cleuch. This is a V-shaped defile of great character with a rather exposed path along the west. At the mouth of the defile a descent can be made to the road at Burn, a route can be made along the upper side of the head dyke to the road, or a cairned route can be followed over Auchenleck Hill back to the start.

# PATHS AND WALKS

*The Enterkin Pass.* The Enterkin Burn rises on Lowther Hill near its col with East Mount Lowther and flows south then south-west to join the River Nith. Until it meets the Nith its considerable course is completely hidden from the outside world by steep hills. The walk up the Enterkin and over its pass is therefore a connoisseur's route with a grand sense of remoteness, though public roads are never very far away.

*The old railway track from Elvanfoot to Wanlockhead*

A right of way starts from the minor road which leaves the A76 at Enterkinfoot and joins the A702 near Durisdeer. Cars can be taken to just north of Muiryhill (875 035). The farm road is taken north, passing east of Inglestone and following the west side of a ridge above the Enterkin Burn. The views are good for so little effort and include the Dalveen as well as the Enterkin Pass. A descent is made to the Enterkin Burn at Glenvalentine where Covenanters are said to have ambushed a party of soldiers and released their captives. The ridges close in here and the path crosses to the west bank to avoid a steep scar. A line of telegraph poles mars the grandeur and leads over the col, but the walk is still impressive. The descent to Wanlockhead is across the western slopes of Lowther Hill joining the route down to the cemetery. (11 kilometres).

*Elvanfoot to Wanlockhead.* The course of the light railway which ran between these villages from 1902 to 1938 can be followed on an attractive elevated walk giving good views to the Lowthers. The walk leaves the A702 at Elvanfoot at an approach road to an electricity sub-station which can be turned on the north side. A two-arch bridge carries the route across the Elvan Water, but a viaduct north of Hass was blown up though it was harming no-one. The Lowthers Railway Society has laid a stretch of narrow gauge track from Leadhills towards Wanlockhead and runs rolling stock on it occasionally. (10 kilometres).

*The Well Path.* This is part of the Roman Road from Nithsdale to Clydesdale. It can be followed from Durisdeer north-eastwards to the A702 east of Troloss. A

*The Well Road from Durisdeer Rig, looking towards Penbane and Well Hill*

modern track takes the east side of the Kirk Burn to the col under Well Hill while the Roman Road is on the west side for the upper part of the route. There is a well preserved Roman fortlet by the road at the foot of Penbane. (7 kilometres).

*Crawfordjohn to Leadhills.* A minor road is followed south to Glentewing where a track is taken to Holmhead and the road up the Snar Water. From Snar Farm a vehicle track is followed above the east bank to Snarhead, or the Snar Water can be left and a route taken south over Reecleuch Hill to the Wanlock Water and Wanlockhead. A number of routes continue from Snarhead to Leadhills. A path from Snarhead follows the Snar Water to cross a col north of Wanlock Dod. This joins a road from Snarhead which has passed east of Hunt Law before dropping to the southern outskirts of Leadhills. A higher path joins this road at Hunt Law while a branch road can be taken from Hunt Law to pass north of a 534m top to drop to the village on a path from the north-west. (13 to 15 kilometres).

*Spango Bridge to Wanlockhead.* This route is a continuation of a route described in Chapter 11. From the B740 it goes south up the east bank of the Wanlock Water past Duntercleuch to Wanlockhead. As a variation, the forest road on the west of the valley can be followed past Clackleith, twisting about until it joins with a variation of the Southern Upland Way west of Duntercleuch Rig to descend to Duntercleuch. (7 or 9 kilometres).

CHAPTER 14

# New Cumnock to Carsphairn

| | | |
|---|---|---|
| **Blackcraig Hill** | 700m | 647 064 |
| **Blacklorg Hill** | 681m | 654 043 |
| **Alhang** | 642m | 642 011 |
| **Windy Standard** | 698m | 620 014 |
| **Moorbrock Hill** | 651m | 620 984 |
| **Cairnsmore of Carsphairn** | 797m | 594 980 |

**ACCESS**

The most useful road into the hills goes south from New Cumnock on the A76 to the Afton Reservoir. The A713 from Dalmellington to Carsphairn brings the opposite side of the range within reach, and offers another approach from this direction along the side road from Lamford to the Water of Deugh. The B729 Carsphairn - Moniaive road sends a branch up the Water of Ken which gives a useful start from the south-east of the range. An eastern approach can be made from Dalgonar on the Scaur Water which is reached from the A702 west of Penpont.

**TRANSPORT**

*Bus:* Kilmarnock to New Cumnock and Dumfries; daily.
Ayr to Carsphairn and Castle Douglas; Monday to Saturday.
Dumfries to Moniaive and Thornhill; daily.

*Train:* Stations at New Cumnock and Kirkconnel.

**ACCOMMODATION**

Hotels at New Cumnock, Sanquhar and Moniaive.
Youth Hostel at Kendoon. Bothies at Clennoch (603 002) and Chalk Memorial (686 019).
Camping at New Cumnock, Cumnock, Sanquhar.

**MAPS**

Ordnance Survey, 1:50,000, Sheet 77

A range of grassy and rounded hills zigzags between the headwaters of the River Nith and the Water of Deugh and Water of Ken following the general north-east to south-west grain of the Southern Uplands. It lies between the Lowther Hills to the north-east and the Galloway Hills to the south-west. The range is contained within a roughly hexagonal shape of roads with the A76 from New Cumnock to Sanquhar and Thornhill and A702 Thornhill to Moniave forming the eastern side and the B729 Moniaive to Carsphairn, A713 Carsphairn to Dalmellington, and B741 Dalmellington to New Cumnock roads forming the boundaries on the south, west and north-west.

The Kello Water, Euchan Water, Scaur Water, Shinnel Water and Dalwhat Water are all eastward-flowing streams which feed the River Nith from this range. Although they flow through sparsely populated territory and are considerable streams covering a large area, there are no very high hills in this eastern sector and forestry is extensive. The hill country becomes more interesting west of the southwards flowing Water of Ken which is on its way to join the River Dee and the Solway Firth. Almost opposite the Ken but slightly more to the west is the northwards flowing Afton Water. This is another tributary of the River Nith which rises much

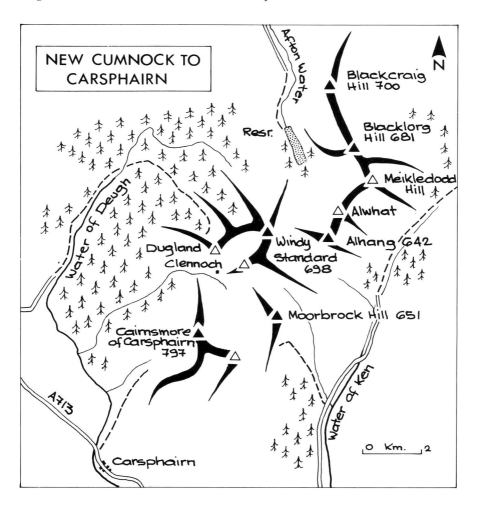

less significantly ten kilometres to the north-west near Dalmellington. The Water of Deugh is the dominant stream in the western sector of the range. It rises only one kilometre from the Afton Water and Nith drainage but pivots in an anti-clockwise turn around the highest hill to join the Water of Ken on its journey south. The banks of the Upper Deugh have been extensively forested, making an approach to the range from the west less attractive to walkers.

Information on the area can be sought in museums or visitor centres at Sanquhar, Dalmellington and Carsphairn.

## THE HILLS

### Blackcraig Hill (700m)
If you drive up the V-shaped Glen Afton from New Cumnock, Blackcraig Hill commands your attention for much of the way. It sits on the east side of the Afton Water and is an unusually rough and craggy hill for this group. A rocky skirt fringes the west side of the hill and is known as the Merry Clints on the north-west and Black Clints on the west. 'The Giant's Cave' between them is prominent from the road, but is only a wet gully and not a cave.

The quickest approach to the hill is from Craig Farm to the west. Park on the Glen Afton road north of Craigdarroch or ask about parking at the water board houses. Follow the road towards Craig over the Afton Water and walk along the south bank past Craig. Cross the Craig Burn and tackle the west slopes of the hill directly. The formidable looking slope is an imposter and any crags are easily turned. Gentler slopes can be found to the south if preferred.

The hill can also be tackled from the bridge over the Afton Water at Blackcraig to the north-west of the hill. This route climbs on grassier slopes avoiding the clints. A number of cairns on the summit ridge are presumably markers for this route, but can be confusing for those coming from the west or south. The summit is marked by a trig point and cairn towards the south end of a broad, stony plateau. A fence east of the summit runs south towards Blacklorg Hill.

### Blacklorg Hill (681m)
This is a much smoother, grassier hill than Blackcraig, and accordingly is duller and less celebrated. Few walkers will climb it on its own, and most will link it with an ascent of Blackcraig Hill or with a round of the hills farther south. Fences between Blackcraig Hill and Meikledodd Hill run over Blacklorg Hill and can be guides in mist though the forest to the east should soon drive people west again. A wall zigzags west to Cannock Hill from Blacklorg Hill and offers an interesting route back to Glen Afton along Craigbraneoch Rig which gives good views over the reservoir. The ridge ends on Craigbraneoch Hill (576m) which is perched above the dam and looks the length of the reservoir to Windy Standard and north down the glen to the Ayrshire plain. It is a superb viewpoint on which to end a day, and is only one kilometre from the road junction at Craig. To avoid the steep cliffs on the north-west face it is best to descend towards the dam and join the water board road.

*Craigbraneoch Hill from Glen Afton*

Those following the main ridge south from Blacklorg Hill follow the fence south-east then south-west to Meikledodd Hill (643m). A fence going south-east from this top leads out along a ridge to Lorg Hill (594m) then descends to the Water of Ken at Lorg, offering an approach line from that side of the hills.

### Alhang (642m)

Alhang sits midway between the Afton Reservoir and the Water of Ken valley and may be climbed from either side. The hill has a lesser top called Alwhat (629m) just over one kilometre to the north. From Alhang a ridge descends to the south-east over a conical spur named Mid Rig. From Alwhat another ridge runs out to the south-east over Ewe Hill which has two tops (575m and 582m) and is quite rugged on its east face. The slopes between these ridges are forested, but an easy round can be made by going up one ridge and down the other. Cars can be taken to the bridge over the Water of Ken at Nether Holm of Dalquhairn and a fence followed onto Ewe Hill from the gate across the road to Lorg. This route gives a fine view to the Galloway Hills down the valley and also shows the Whigs Hole (670 000) on Altry Hill across the river, which was reputedly used by Covenanters as a hide-out.

If approaching Alhang from the north on the main ridge, a fence marks the high ground and regional boundary from Blackcraig Hill and Blacklorg Hill. The source of the Afton Water is passed in the col between Alwhat and Alhang and the ridge gives a good view to Glen Afton and its reservoir from there. The summit of the hill is marked by a few boulders while the fence turns north-west towards Windy Standard.

**Windy Standard** (698m)
The slightly tilted table top appearance of this hill is a distinguishing feature, with the summit slope sliding gently into a steeper trapezial outline. This view is well seen from the road between Cumnock and New Cumnock. The grassy hill sits two and a half kilometres south-west of the Afton Reservoir and is normally climbed from the water works there. Although a water board road contours much of the reservoir, it is cut off from the open slopes by an almost unbroken barrier of conifers. It is wise to get above the trees at the dam where a rocky outcrop is known as Castle William. A ridge is followed over Wedder Hill and Millmaneoch Hill before the north-east ridge of Windy Standard is reached and a short traverse leads to a direct line for the summit trig point. There is a wind charger and semi-underground chamber nearby.

   The hill can also be reached from the A713 at Meadowhead by driving to the bridge over the Water of Deugh under Brownhill Rig. Continue from a gate along the east bank road past Brownhill and Moor. The road splits under the bold, rocky Craignane (502m) which gives a fine view down the valley. Take the road on its south side towards Dun Hill and climb by a firebreak to open slopes on Polwhat Rig. Turn east from the Rig to Trostan Hill and a slight drop leads to Windy Standard.

   A long north-west ridge leads from Windy Standard to Jedburgh Knees (621m) which does not qualify as a Donald top. Dugland (608m) south-west of Trostan Hill and Keoch Rig (610m), two kilometres along the south ridge of Windy Standard both rank as tops and are awkward to reach from most directions. Dugland stands above a rebuilt Clennoch bothy. The south ridge from Windy Standard leads past the Deil's Putting Stone, which is a large boulder with a giant thumbhole in it. A fence continues down this ridge to the Keoch Rig. The Blue Stones on the east face of the hill are steep screes which give a good view of the 'basket of eggs' drumlins crowding the upper Holm Burn valley.

   A round from Craigengillan in the Ken valley can include Moorbrock Hill, Windy Standard and the ridge to the south-east over Mid Hill of Glenhead and Dodd Hill, which has a sizeable lochan at its summit.

**Moorbrock Hill** (651m)
The distinctive shape of this hill catches the eye from the south. The steep V-shaped pass between Moorbrock Hill and Beninner is like a miniature Lairig Ghru and is a reliable landmark in the rolling countryside. The shortest route to the hill starts from Craigengillan to the south on the Water of Ken. There is room for a car or two at the road junction provided access for lorries is kept clear. Walk up the farm road to

*Cairnsmore of Carsphairn from the Water of Deugh*

Moorbrock and continue on it past the farm through a line of drumlins as it heads straight for the hill. This road was extended in the early 1980s for mineral exploration on Moorbrock Hill. It contours across Green Hill then climbs behind it to the summit ridge of Moorbrock Hill. Walkers are quicker ascending the Poltie Burn to meet another limb of the road which is being rapidly eroded away.

The summit of the hill is towards the north end of a level grassy ridge with a steep scree face falling to the east, the Moorbrock Gairy. The ridge continues on a north-west bend, falling slightly, then rises to an elevation little lower than the main summit. Luke's Stone in the col to the north is an unimpressive boulder.

**Cairnsmore of Carsphairn** (797m)
The highest hill in the range is also the highest of three Cairnsmores in South-West Scotland which are sometimes tackled in one expedition by masochists. Cairnsmore of Carsphairn is a shapely hill from the south along with its subsidiary top, Beninner. Both hills have steep scree faces to the east. The Gairy on Beninner is particularly distinctive in views from afar.

Cairnsmore on its own is a fairly easy walk from the Carsphairn side, but forests on the north and west complicate ascents from these directions, while hills to the east get in the way of a direct assault from the Ken Valley. The simplest route leaves the A713 north of Carsphairn at the Green Well of Scotland. This is a rocky gorge which offers fine views to the hill along the river from a grove of pines and deciduous trees. The route goes up the east bank of the Water of Deugh starting from the house by the bridges. A vehicle track leads across a level strath past cattle sheds to cross the Benloch Burn. The track leaves the Deugh there and is followed uphill in a north-east direction under the western slopes of Willieanna and Dunool. The latter marks the start of an L-shaped ridge to Cairnsmore round a shallow west-facing corrie. The road runs to the lip of this corrie at 420m where a stone wall is met and followed north-eastwards to the summit cairn near the trig point. A smaller cairn to the north marks the start of the north ridge.

The southern and western slopes of Cairnsmore are grassy and rounded, but the northern and eastern sides are more rugged and show underlying granite. The summit ridge becomes stony as it goes north from Black Shoulder until it falls away steeply more than one kilometre north of the summit in a landscape of slabs and perched boulders. Some of the erratics on the northern half of the hill are of considerable size. There is a huge scone-shaped stone on the north ridge, while others to the north-east below the gairy can provide rude shelter.

Beninner (710m) is a south-east top with a small cairn. It has a smooth summit cap with only a few small stones showing through the vegetation. If returning to the Green Well from Beninner, beware of an electric fence running along the top of the march dyke where it runs south from Willieanna to cross the Benloch Burn. It is simpler to rejoin the ridge south of Cairnsmore and drop down the Black Shoulder past a little lochan to Dunool, Willieanna and the road to the west.

*Looking down the Water of Deugh to the Rhinns of Carsphairn*

   Cairnsmore and Beninner can also be climbed from Knockgray near Carsphairn or from Craigengillan in the valley of the Water of Ken. The Knockgray approach under Quantans Hill is rather dull, but the view from Craig of Knockgray which sits to the west is very fine over Carsphairn to the Galloway Hills. From Craigengillan the rough road is followed past Moorbrock and the west side of Green Hill to reach the impressively steep gairy on Beninner. A direct route can be taken up the steep slopes, or the gairy can be turned on the north or south.

# CHAPTER 15

# The North Galloway Hills

| | | |
|---|---|---|
| **Coran of Portmark** | 623m | 509 937 |
| **Meaul** | 695m | 500 910 |
| **Cairnsgarroch** | 659m | 515 914 |
| **Carlin's Cairn** | 807m | 497 883 |
| **Corserine** | 814m | 498 870 |
| **Milldown** | 738m | 511 839 |
| **Meikle Millyea** | 746m | 518 829 |
| **Craiglee** (Loch Doon) | 523m | 471 963 |
| **Macaterick** | 499m | 438 900 |
| **Mullwharchar** | 692m | 454 866 |
| **Dungeon Hill** | 610m | 460 851 |
| **Craignaw** | 645m | 459 833 |
| **Craiglee** (Loch Dee) | 531m | 462 801 |
| **Shalloch on Minnoch** | 775m | 407 906 |
| **Tarfessock** | 696m | 409 892 |
| **Kirriereoch Hill** | 786m | 421 870 |
| **Merrick** | 843m | 428 855 |

The North Galloway Hills stretch in three parallel ranges between Loch Doon and the gap separating Glen Trool from Loch Dee and Clatteringshaws Loch. The three ranges are aligned north to south with the central granite range overshadowed by the higher outer ranges. Lower ridges aligned roughly west to east lie to the north of the Trool-Dee Gap and west of Loch Doon completing an aureole around the granite cauldron which has caused considerable metamorphosis in the surrounding rocks.

The eastern range is a long unbroken chain for some 17 kilometres and is known as the Rhinns of Carsphairn and Kells. The Dungeon Range in the granite core of the district is named after one of its hills and three lochs at its foot. The western range can show an eerie resemblance to a gigantic hand when seen from the air and is known as the Awful Hand.

The ranges have an abundance of lochs trapped in their glacial hollows and the area could well be described as the lake or loch district of Southern Scotland. Some of the lochs are used for public water supply to distant towns and some for hydro-electric purposes in a scheme spanning the Glenkens to the east. Water from

## ACCESS

Three roads in the shape of a truncated triangle give access to this district. At points on these roads, from north, east, south and west, motorists may drive nearer to the hills. From the A713 Dalmellington to New Galloway road, branches go off to the foot of Loch Doon and from Polharrow Bridge to Forrest Lodge. From the A762 and A712 between Earlstoun Loch and Clatteringshaws Loch, branches go west up the Garroch Glen to Drumbuie and north of Clatteringshaws Loch to a junction past Upper Craigenbay. A branch from the A712 takes the south and west shore of the latter loch to just past Craigencallie. The road into Glen Trool is the most popular approach, leaving the unclassified hill road running from the A714 between Bargrennan and Straiton. A branch from this hill road can also be driven from Stinchar Bridge to Ballochbeatties south of Loch Bradan. In addition private roads may be walked from the A713 at Drumjohn, Brochloch, and beyond Holm of Daltallochan over the Carsphairn Lane to the Garryhorn Lead Mines west of Carsphairn, and west of Polmaddie to the east slopes of Carlin's Cairn, while farm and forest roadsfrom the Bargrennan-Straiton road lead into the hills at Gleckmalloch, Kirriereoch, Tarfessock (by ford), and Laglanny.

## TRANSPORT

*Bus:* Ayr to Dalmellington and Castle Douglas; Monday to Saturday.
Ayr to Glentrool and Newton Stewart; daily.

*Train:* Station at Barrhill.

## ACCOMMODATION

Hotels at Bargrennan, Dalry, New Galloway, Newton Stewart and Barrhill.
Youth Hostels at Kendoon and Minnigaff.
Camping at Glentrool, Bargrennan, Newton Stewart, Talnotry under Murray's Monument on A712, and Parton. Bothies at Culsharg (415 821), White Laggan (466 774), Back Hill of Bush (480 843), Shiel of Castlemaddy (539 901), Tunskeen (424 906) and Cross Burn - the Wigwam (389 879).

## MAPS

Ordnance Survey 1:50,000, Sheet 77
Harvey 1:40,000, Galloway Hills, Glen Trool
Bartholomew 1:100,000, Stranraer and Galloway

Loch Doon is piped through the Rhinns of Carsphairn to divert it to the Deugh, Ken and Dee, with dams and power stations exploiting the gradients at Drumjohn, Kendoon, Carsfad, Earlstoun, Clatteringshaws and Glenlee, and Tongland. Small power schemes have also been developed on the Forrest Estate east of the Rhinns of Kells.

A large forest covers much of the Forrest Estate. The Galloway Forest Park is a neighbour to the west, north and south taking in the Awful Hand and Dungeon Ranges and the western slopes of the Rhinns of Carsphairn and Kells. While the high ridges are clear of trees, access to them is hampered in many areas by the plantations, so forest roads need to be followed. Forest trails have been established at Glen Trool and Stinchar Bridge and a visitor centre at Clatteringshaws. The Bruce's Stone east of Clatteringshaws Loch commemorates a battle of 1307.

A road goes north-west from the Straiton-Bargrennan road at Rowantree Toll and passes through the scenic Nick of the Balloch to Barr. Craigenreoch (565m), south-west of the summit of this road, gives a good view of the Awful Hand Range and can be crossed in a short ridge walk which includes Pinbreck and Haggis Hill. Numerous walks can be made in this area between Barrhill and Barr, and Pinwherry and Rowantree Toll, but most involve forest roads and firebreaks now. There are no hills of distinction beyond this to the west except for the miniatures of Byne Hill (214m) at Girvan and Knockdolian (265m) near Ballantrae.

## THE HILLS

**Coran of Portmark** (623m)
This is the most northerly Donald in the Rhinns of Carsphairn. It and its smaller northern neighbour, Black Craig, stand like two huge drumlins at the north end of the range between Carsphairn and Loch Doon and may be climbed from both directions.

From Green Well of Scotland the road west to Garryhorn is taken (leaving cars on the A713 as there is no room to park or turn on the side road). The road goes through the farm to the Woodhead lead mines which operated between 1838 and 1873 producing lead, silver and other minerals. A peak population of about 300 lived there, but now the village is scanty and ruined. A two-storey schoolhouse, rows of houses and a building adapted as a shooting lodge can be seen. From the smelter site opposite this lodge, a crumbling underground duct leads uphill to a flue chimney. Shafts up to 50m deep have been filled in, but one still gapes at the sky inside a fence. Lazy beds, a small reservoir and a lade can still be traced.

The route to the hills passes through a gate in a wall above the highest row of houses and turns north to pass through a gate in a fence and climb across the slopes of Knockower to the cairn on the main hill.

From Loch Head at the foot of Loch Doon, the route is barred by forest. By going up a ride by the Loch Head Burn another break appears heading north-east which leads out to the Meaul-Bow col. Bow is the south top of Coran of Portmark and has a stony ridge with three rises of which the north is the highest. A fence from Coran of Portmark runs over Bow and south down its ridge.

Roads from Drumjohn and Brochloch can also be used to reach the hill. Both roads join east of Craigencolon which is a superb viewpoint. A track from Lamloch in the same area runs to the lead mines past the ruins of a free church used by the miners. A monument on Garryhorn Rig at (538 944) commemorates David McMath, a gamekeeper from the mines, who perished in a snowstorm in 1925.

**Meaul** (695m)
This hill may be climbed from Loch Doon or Carsphairn with Coran of Portmark and Bow. The fence from Bow meets a wall coming up from the east at the start of the north ridge to Meaul. An upright stone on this ridge to the west of the fence

*Carlin's Cairn and Meaul from Bow*

commemorates John Dempster, a Covenanter who was shot there. The slope gives a view of Loch Doon from end to end. Meaul has a grassy north ridge, a bouldery summit, and a south ridge which descends from a zone of grey outcropping stones to one of smaller and darker shaly fragments and then grass again at the south col, where there are a number of lochans.

From the summit trig point on Meaul, a wall descends the east shoulder of the hill and meets the fence from Bow before dropping to the col to Cairnsgarroch. The King's Well is a spring just west of the col. Three chair-shaped stones are grouped around a table stone at the King's Seat beside the well and are traditionally associated with Robert the Bruce.

### Cairnsgarroch (659m)

This is an outlying hill east of the Rhinns of Carsphairn. It is usually climbed from Meaul or the lead mines. A cairn at the summit sits south of the wall coming from Meaul. A direct route can be made to the hill from the lead mines but the Garryhorn Burn has to be crossed. This area and the slopes around Craighit are enclosed by electric fencing carrying very high voltages so it is essential to use the gates provided. An old mine adit can be seen above Craighit (525 925). The Lumps of Garryhorn north of the hill are morainic mounds.

## Carlin's Cairn (807m)

A narrow ridge above steep slopes and a massive summit cairn make this probably the most memorable hill in the range. The cairn is said to have been erected by an old woman in honour of Robert the Bruce, but it probably dates from the Bronze Age. The quickest route to the hill starts from Loch Doon and follows the forest road which heads south to the east of the Gala Lane. Where the road turns west, a firebreak leads east towards the north ridge of the hill. The outcrop scenery on this ridge above the Goat Craigs is startling, with a clear dividing line between the rugged pink granite and the overlying black shale which is splintered into small fragments. A similar transition can be seen on the ridge south of the summit accompanied by thin layers of upended strata.

Coming from Meaul, the ridge has a kink to the east at the Goat Craigs, then bends south-west over a false top before heading south to the real summit. A long forest road leads in to the hill from the A713 at Polmaddie past Castlemaddy. An old drove road from the Girvan valley passed the south end of Loch Doon and crossed the col between Meaul and Carlin's Cairn to Shiel of Castlemaddy, but it is now lost in the forest.

## Corserine (814m)

This is the second highest hill in Galloway and sits midway between Loch Doon and Loch Dee near the middle of its range. Four ridges cross at its summit as its name tells. The east ridge further divides into north-east and south-east branches which form headwalls for unfloored corrie formations to the north and east. The valleys to the north-west and south-east of the summit also have cirque shapes, but are more

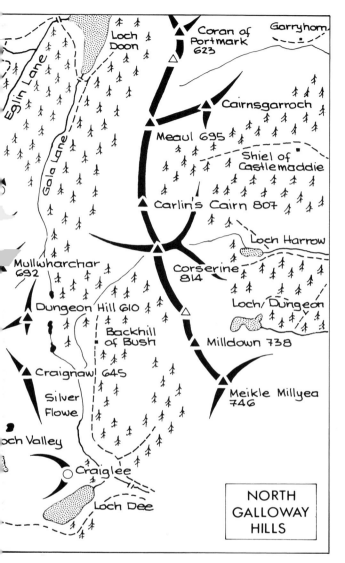

grassy. The five ridges give the hill a star-shaped plan, but the main mass is a bulky whale-back cloaked in grass over much of its slopes. The summit vegetation is severely stunted and is interspersed with bare, stony patches where any rocks uncovered are quickly broken down to gravel sized frag-ments. The lower ground to east and west is heavily forested.

The hill may best be reached from the Polharrow Glen where there is a car park near Forrest Lodge. A kilted figure from an Olsen Line ship stands guard at the gate to the lodge. Take the road west on the south side of the Polharrow Burn past Fore Bush and continue from a junc-tion along the south side of Loch Harrow. This continues west as a firebreak and leads to the rocky North Gairy Top (681m) and a long gentle south-east ridge. The right fork in the road can also be taken to a fire-break leading onto the north-east ridge above Polmaddy Gairy, which joins with the first route and leads to the summit plateau with its trig point.

If the hill is climbed from Loch Doon, the forest road east of the Gala Lane can be fol-lowed until it turns sharply west. The more easterly of two firebreaks leads in an east of south direction over the Kirreoch Burn to a road which turns the Riders Rig from the south. Cross the road and continue up a ride through the trees to Meikle Craigtarson. The top of this ridge is quite stony and leads east by grassy slopes up to Corserine.

If Corserine is taken in a traverse of the main ridge from north or south, the ascent is simple on grassy slopes.

*Milldown and Loch Dungeon from North Gairy Top*

**Milldown** (738m)

This hill lies south from Corserine. It has very steep rocky slopes to the east and large forests farther east and to the west, where they rise high up the north-western slope. Accordingly, the hill is usually climbed along the ridge from Corserine or Meikle Millyea. The route from the south follows a wall past the Lochans of Auchniebut in the col below Meikle Millyea. Milldown has a small cairn east of the wall with an airy drop below down the dark shaly crags to the appropriately named Loch Dungeon. The view west extends past the Dungeon Range to Merrick and can show the Lion's Head shape of Dungeon Hill particularly well.

A narrow bouldery ridge drops gradually to the north and rises to a north top - Millfire (716m). A route from the col between them leads west through the forest down to Backhill of Bush and can be used on an approach starting from Clattering-shaws Loch in the south.

When the Back Bush was occupied, the pony track to the outside world lay over the col at 628m between Corserine and Millfire on a route to the Fore Bush. A memorial stands inside a dry stone enclosure between Millfire and Loch Harrow on the east side of the Hawse Burn to Ralph Forlow, a shepherd who perished there in snow in 1954. A bridge over the Hawse Burn leads east by a firebreak past the memorial to join a forest road between Loch Minnoch and Loch Dungeon which leads to the road at Burnhead. The banks of the Hawse Burn are dotted with

*Corserine to Meikle Millyea and Loch Dungeon*

drumlins which form a transition landscape between the crags of Millfire and the smooth slopes of Corserine.

### Meikle Millyea (746m)

This is the southernmost Donald of the Rhinns of Kells. It can be climbed from Craigencallie to the south or in a round with Corserine from Forrest Glen. From Craigencallie west of Clatteringshaws Loch, a forest road runs north-west to branch across the River Dee where a firebreak can be taken to Darrou (470m). After a slight drop the route climbs to Little Millyea (579m). Both give good views. The ridge continues north under grass and is followed up a wall to the mossy plateau of Meikle Millyea where the summit is distinguished by a trig point and large cairn at the north end.

If coming to the hill from the Polharrow Glen, the road south-west is taken from the car park past Burnhead. Disregard a road going north to Loch Dungeon and Loch Minnoch and continue south-west in the valley of McAdam's Burn. A firebreak from the end of the road leads south clear of the forest. Go west with the wall along the edge of the forest and climb the rough slopes to the north-east ridge of Meikle Millyea which is an excellent viewpoint for the range to Corserine. The wall running up the ridge from there uses massive boulders from the abundant supply scattered around.

**Craiglee** (523m), Loch Doon

This little hill sits between Loch Finlas and the south end of Loch Doon. It can be climbed from the Loch Doon road near the castle or farther north beyond a plantation. The route goes over Wee Hill of Craigmulloch (421m) which is one of the finest viewpoints in Southern Scotland.

The hill may also be reached by following a forest road south of the Garpel Burn to the open slopes above Loch Finlas and following the burn up to the Nick of the Loup. The views from the two hills look to the big hills of Galloway and Loch Doon, where from time to time the castle island appears above the water. This was the original site of the castle before the level of the loch was raised and the castle was re-erected on the west bank.

**Macaterick** (499m)

Because of its small height and remoteness, this is probably the least climbed hill in these Galloway ranges. It lies south-west of Loch Doon and is the culmination of a low ridge running northwards from Kirriereoch Hill. The hill is less than an hour from Tunskeen Bothy, and both can be visited on the same route which starts as a forest road at the south-west end of Loch Doon. This follows the north bank of the Carrick Lane to Loch Riecawr and a branch road west of this loch to the ruin of Slaethornrig. The edge of the forest is followed to Tunskeen and the Tunskeen Lane crossed to reach Macaterick.

This is rugged granite territory and very coarse vegetation sprouting from the poorly drained soil makes it a tiring route. Loch Macaterick lies immediately below the very broken northern slopes of the hill. A return can be made to Loch Doon in a north-easterly direction provided the shallows of the Black Garpel can be crossed, linking up with a route to Mullwharchar.

**Mullwharchar** (692m)

The highest of the granite Dungeon Range hills became famous in 1976 when it was disclosed that the nuclear industry was interested in burying nuclear waste in it. After a prolonged campaign and a public inquiry objectors fended off the proposal, but not before an odd assortment of commoners, media experts and professional bagmen had stumbled around the area.

There are no easy routes to the hill as it is centrally placed in a wilderness between Loch Doon and Loch Trool. From the south-west end of Loch Doon one route follows the forest road north of the Carrick Lane to a bridge over the Whitespout Lane east of the ruin at Craigfionn. South of the bridge a branch in the road is taken east and south until a wide firebreak leads east to a bridge over the Eglin Lane. An alternative is to follow the forest road south from Loch Doon on the east side of the Gala Lane. This eventually swings west and leads to a bridge over the Gala Lane. The north ridge of Hoodens Hill is quite narrow and leads to a level walk on granite pavements over Lump of the Eglin and a descent past two small lochans to the final rise to Mullwharchar.

*Mullwharchar from the Gala Lane*

The east face of the hill is very craggy in terraced precipices at The Slock, Yellow Tomach and The Tauchers. From Glen Trool a round of Loch Enoch can take in Craignaw, Dungeon Hill, Mullwharchar and Merrick. The Eglin Lane is normally crossable at the outlet from Loch Enoch.

### Dungeon Hill (610m)

Like a reclining lion, Dungeon Hill broods over the watershed between the Clyde and the Solway in the far-off reaches of a great valley. The shortest route to the hill is probably from Glen Trool following the west side of the Gairland Burn and east shore of Loch Neldricken to a prominent cairn in the col north of Craignaw, the Nick of the Dungeon. A rising bee-line to the north-east leads to the west face of the hill where outcrops are easily turned.

Looking across Loch Enoch to Mullwharchar

The watery channels of the Silver Flowe, a National Nature Reserve, are conspicuous on the moor below beyond the Round and Long Lochs of the Dungeon. The Dry Loch of the Dungeon is over the watershed to the north in an area where there are some mighty boulders on the slopes of Dungeon Hill.

If an ascent of the hill is made from Craigencallie following the forest road to Back Hill of Bush, a firebreak west leads to a boggy route between the Long and Round Lochs to the foot of Dungeon Hill. A route to the north past the Dungeon Stone and Dry Loch leads to the foot of the north ridge of Dungeon Hill which is called The Brishie. This is a narrow scenic way to the summit reminiscent of Arran. A round from Loch Doon over Mullwharchar and Dungeon Hill can return by this north ridge and a long firebreak to a forest road, but it is a wearisome plod beneath the hills.

### Craignaw (645m)
One of the finest walks in the Southern Uplands leaves Glen Trool at the end of the road, descends to Buchan past the Buchan Falls and takes a slanting path across Buchan Hill to the lip of a hanging valley out of which tumbles the Gairland Burn. The west bank of Loch Valley is passed and the Mid Burn crossed between it and Loch Neldricken. A climb to the east leaves the coarse grass behind and gives a grand slabby walk north to Craignaw. It is a splendid little mountain bristling with granite.

*Craignaw from Dungeon Hill*

Below the summit to the south-west a lighter patch on the grey face shows where an F1-11 fighter plane came to grief above the Black Gairy. This line of crags continues north of the summit giving a big step down to the north-west ridge. A steep heathery descent leads to this level ridge where boulders were strewn in chaos by the melting glaciers. One level platform is known as the De'ils Bowling Green from the arrangement of rounded boulders arrayed on it. At the Nick of the Dungeon at the north end of the ridge, routes east lead to Backhill of Bush, north to Dungeon Hill, and south-west to Loch Neldricken.

The ridge south-east from Craignaw passes Dow Loch which sends the Dow Spout cascading down a line of crags to the Cooran Lane. Snibe Hill at the south end of this ridge is very rocky but can be descended to the south-east to the Cooran Lane which is dark and deep but normally crossable at a ford where it turns north near Ellergower Knowe.

**Craiglee** (531m), Loch Dee
Another rough granite hill belies its modest height. With Loch Trool to the west, Loch Dee and Clatteringshaws Loch to the east, several lochs of its own and a number of lochs to the north, it is a superb viewpoint. The hill can be climbed from Craigencallie by following the road from Clatteringshaws Loch round the south of Loch Dee and climbing the south ridge.

From Glen Trool the path up the Gairland Burn is taken to cross the burn near Loch Valley (which can be difficult) and ascend the Rig of the Jarkness. The Dow Loch sits in a hollow on this ridge. A descent can be made between the two lochs of Glenhead to Glen Trool.

### Shalloch on Minnoch (775m)
The most westerly Corbett and Donald in the Southern Uplands stands south-west of Loch Doon and east of the hill road going south from Straiton. It is easily climbed from the summit of this road at 433m, though a north top (659m) has to be climbed first. The eastern face is more scarped and interesting and can be reached from Loch Doon by the forest road past Loch Riecawr to near Slaethornrig. There are two rises on the stony summit plateau. The main summit is 300 metres south-east of the trig point.

If more than one hill in the range is to be visited, a start can be made from the car park near Rowantree Toll (353 908) where Davie Bell, a local cyclist and writer, is commemorated. Go down the burnside to Laglanny and follow the road past the bungalow at Shalloch on Minnoch. Continue up the Shalloch Burn, cross a bridge and slant up a firebreak to slopes west of the summit.

### Tarfessock (696m)
This hill is usually climbed along with Shalloch on Minnoch over the V-shaped Nick of Carclach. From there the north ridge is ascended past an interesting contrast of dark-grey outcrops and grey-white erratics. A cairn of white quartzite boulders marks the north-west end of the hill, while the main summit sits at the south end beyond a little lochan. The ground to the south of the hill is very irregular and runs as a long exposed ridge to Kirriereoch Hill. Tarfessock has a south top (620m) at the north end of this area. Pink, dark grey and light grey rocks surface, adjoin or decorate the disordered slopes here where the metamorphic aureole is in evidence.

A start can be made to this range from the Straiton-Bargrennan road at a picnic place on the Water of Minnoch (359 867). A forest road is followed east to Kirriereoch Loch then north towards the house called Kirriereoch. Turn east away from the access road, ignore access roads going right to Kirriemore and left to Tarfessock and continue on the main route north-east. The road turns east towards the hills then north across the Pillow Burn and east again to its end about 200 metres north of Cross Burn Bothy. A muddy break through the trees leads to the bothy and a route up the burn to Tarfessock. The hill can also be reached from a route north of there into Shalloch on Minnoch by taking the Knocklach Burn.

### Kirriereoch Hill (786m)
The hill is remote from Glen Trool and Loch Doon but may be climbed from the Straiton-Bargrennan road by the route described to Tarfessock past Cross Burn Bothy. The east bank of the burn is followed downstream until clear of the trees and a ridge climbed south-east past Carnirock Stone, which is a large erratic. Old fence posts and the remains of a wall lead up the grassy ridge on the regional boundary and pass slightly north of the summit cairn.

*Merrick from Mullwharchar*

Balminnoch Loch nestles closely under the hill on its north side. Steep bouldery slopes lead down this northern face and can look quite intimidating. The slope is normally easy but requires care. Easier grassy slopes to the south lead past outcrops and erratics to the col under the impressive northern spur of Merrick. Loch Twachtan is a round little tarn below this col to the east. Kirriereoch Hill is linked to Tarfessock by a broad band of broken ground in the form of a ridge with numerous lochans, bluffs, depressions, outcrops and boulders. A fence crosses the south end of this ridge under Kirriereoch Hill.

### Merrick (843m)

The Merrick, as it is usually called in foremost respect, is the highest hill in the Southern Uplands. As a result it is often visited, and is an easy climb from Glen Trool to the south.

A path leaves the upper car park at the end of the road, near the boulder commemorating Robert the Bruce's victory in 1307 over an English force, and goes up the west side of the Buchan Burn. The burn is picturesque as it tumbles in cataracts from a hanging valley into the oakwoods of Buchan. Beyond a stile, the path leaves the burn for a shelf above and enters the forest to pass through to the partly restored ruin of Culsharg. Behind the house, the path takes off upwards to cross a forest road and a bridge and continue up north-westwards to open slopes. A fence is crossed and a wall followed up to the cairn on Benyellary (719m).

*Shalloch on Minnoch from the forest road to Loch Riecawr*

*Loch Trool and Benyellary from Mulldonach*

*Merrick from Craig Neldricken across Loch Enoch*

The major summit should now be seen two kilometres to the north-east across a narrow col. The wall leads on across the col to the steep north face of Merrick and is a good guide to the edge of the cliffs in mist. The path leaves the north side of the col and slants up in a more direct line to the large cairn and trig point on the summit.

Embedded boulders stud the summit slopes, partly sunken due to frost-heaving of the soil. The view stretches from the Lake District and Mountains of Mourne to the Crianlarich Hills. A narrow and distinctive north ridge known as the Spear or Fang of the Merrick drops steeply from the summit, levels off briefly, then drops again to a col with Kirriereoch Hill.

An interesting route back to Glen Trool starts with a descent of the east ridge where outcrops show a transition from black shaly rocks to lighter granite. The views are very fine with the little loch in an island on Loch Enoch prominent. In the valley of the Buchan Burn, the Grey Man of the Merrick is an outcrop showing the shape of a bearded man when seen from the east (437 846).

If returning from Loch Enoch, follow the valley floor until Benyellary appears and you should find the outcrop on the west side of the valley. The route back to Glen Trool lies along the Rig of Loch Enoch and over Buchan Hill for fine views, or by the less interesting route down the Buchan Burn.

# CHAPTER 16

# The South Galloway Hills

| | | |
|---|---|---|
| **Larg Hill** | 676m | 424 758 |
| **Lamachan Hill** | 716m | 435 770 |
| **Curleywee** | 674m | 454 770 |
| **Millfore** | 656m | 478 755 |
| **Cairnsmore of Fleet** | 711m | 501 671 |
| **Cairnsmore of Dee** | 493m | 584 758 |
| **Criffel** | 569m | 957 618 |
| **Screel Hill** | 343m | 779 553 |
| **Bengairn** | 391m | 770 545 |

In the last chapter the gap between Loch Trool and Loch Dee and Clatteringshaws Loch was used to mark the southern boundary for the three northern ranges of Galloway. This chapter deals with the hills south of that line. A fourth range, known as the Lamachans or Minnigaff Hills, is tightly contained south of the Trool-Dee-Clatteringshaws Gap, but south of that range the hills are much more widely spread between the Cree and Nith estuaries. A large area of wild country south of the A712 from Newton Stewart to New Galloway can only produce one Donald in Cairnsmore of Fleet, while Bengairn and Screel Hill near Palnackie and Criffel near Kirkbean are isolated hill masses.

The Lamachan Range and some of the ground south of the A712 forms part of the Galloway Forest Park with visitor centres at Clatteringshaws on the A712 and Kirroughtree off the A75 at Palnure. There are forest trails at Kirroughtree, Glen Trool, Talnotry, Clatteringshaws and areas to the south, and forest drives at Kirroughtree and Clatteringshaws. Along the A712 between Clatteringshaws and Talnotry there are wild goat and red deer parks, where animals harmful to forestry interests have been granted their own reserves and can usually be seen from the road.

The tall obelisk on a hillock at Talnotry is a memorial to Alexander Murray (1775-1813) professor of oriental languages at Edinburgh University. The ruins of his birthplace where he started life as a shepherd may be visited across the Palnure Burn from the goat park. West of Craigdews Hill and the goat park the Grey Mare's Tail Burn runs under the road at a car park. The walk up the burn from here passes some fine waterfalls.

## ACCESS
The northern hills in this chapter can be reached from Glen Trool off the A714 Newton Stewart to Barrhill road or from Craigencallie west of Clatteringshaws Loch on the A712 Newton Stewart to New Galloway road. In addition a minor road leads off the A712 at Craigdews to Black Loch, while north from the A712 and the B7079 near Newton Stewart minor roads join to run up the Penkiln Burn to Auchinleck. The A712 also gives access to Cairnsmore of Fleet and Cairsmore of Dee on its south side. The former can also be reached from the A75 Newton Stewart to Creetown road or the hill road which becomes the B796 between Creetown and Gatehouse of Fleet. Criffel is easily reached from the A710 between New Abbey and Kirkbean. Screel Hill and Bengairn can be reached from the B727 or A711 Kirkcudbright to Dalbeattie roads.

## TRANSPORT
*Bus:* Ayr to Glentrool and Newton Stewart; daily.
Ayr to Castle Douglas; Monday to Saturday.
Stranraer to Gatehouse of Fleet, Castle Douglas and Dumfries; daily.
Dumfries to Rockcliffe; daily.

*Postbus:* Castle Douglas to Auchencairn; Monday to Saturday.
Castle Douglas to Mossdale and Bennan; Monday to Saturday.

## ACCOMMODATION
Hotels at Bargrennan, New Galloway, Newton Stewart, Castle Douglas, Dalry, Creetown, Gelston, Auchencairn, Gatehouse of Fleet, New Abbey, Dalbeattie, Mabie, Kirkbean, Rockcliffe and Sandyhills.
Youth hostels at Kendoon and Minnigaff.
Bothy at White Laggan (466 774).
Camping at Glentrool, Bargrennan, Talnotry under Murray's Monument on A712, Newton Stewart, Castle Douglas, Dalbeattie, Kippford, Palnackie, Gatehouse of Fleet, Beeswing, Kirkcudbright and Southerness.

## MAPS
Ordnance Survey 1:50,000, Sheets 77, 83 and 84
Harvey 1:40,000, Galloway Hills, Glen Trool
Bartholomew 1:100,000, Stranraer and Galloway

There is much fine coastal scenery along the Solway coast with particularly impressive cliffs at the Mull of Galloway, Burrow Head and Port o' Warren.


# THE HILLS

### Larg Hill (676m)
Three hills south of the Trool-Dee Gap are usually climbed together from Glen Trool or the Penkiln Glen to the south. Larg Hill is the most westerly of the three. Forests stretch west and north between it and Glen Trool and south-east between it and the Penkiln Glen. Nevertheless it can be easily reached from the Penkiln Glen by following the forest road from Garlick (447 705). This follows the glen for five kilometres past the ruin at Lamachan until a firebreak leads up the slope to the hill.

*Lamachan Hill, with Larg Hill to its left, from Curleywee*

From Glen Trool a route leaves the Caldons camp site and follows the west bank of the Caldons Burn up past a fine gorge until, once clear of the forest, a way is made south up to the summit. A much longer route from this camp site follows the forest road which goes west of Jenny's Hill and Craignaw to pass between Craigenroy and Loch Middle, where a firebreak and wall will be found leading up from the south-west to the summit ridge over a 658m rise. This wall leads on down to the col under Lamachan Hill.

### Lamachan Hill (716m)
This is the highest point of the crescent-shaped ridge which connects the three Donalds of this group. The hill may be climbed from Glen Trool by the Caldons Burn or from the Penkiln Glen by taking the same routes as for Larg Hill. If coming from Larg Hill a line of old fence posts can aid navigation in mist. On the north side of this line a curious erratic is shaped like a quartered bun. The cairn on Lamachan Hill sits at the south end of the summit cap. A ridge running north-west from the summit drops from Cambrick Hill to the Nick of the Lochans and then rises again over the rugged Mulldonach (557m). The views can be excellent on this ridge, which is another route to or from Glen Trool, but it has a short steep and arduous section among the trees above the path at the east end of Loch Trool.

The route to Lamachan Hill from the Nick of Curleywee follows a path on the north side of the ridge to Bennanbrack on the rim of a corrie ringed with shaly

*Curleywee and Lamachan Hill from the path to Benyellary above Culsharg bothy*

outcrops. Gentle grassy slopes then lead south-west to the summit at the end of a wall coming up from the west. The ruins of an old fence lead from Curleywee over Lamachan Hill to Larg Hill.

### Curleywee (674m)
This is one of the finest hills in the Southern Uplands. With its distinctive cone shape, and steep slopes riven with scars and screes of black shale, it has a unique character among the whalebacks of the south. Its peaked summit is the centre point of a north-south ridge running from White Hill to Bennan Hill at right angles to the main Lamachan Range ridge.

The simplest approach to Curleywee is from Craigencallie near Clatteringshaws. By walking the forest road to the south end of Loch Dee a way can be made from White Laggan up the burn to the west directly to the summit.

A route from Glen Trool starts at the upper car park and goes past Buchan towards Glenhead. Just before Glenhead a bridge leads across the Glenhead Burn onto the Southern Upland Way, which is followed along the edge of the forest then up a branch of the burn onto a road to Loch Dee. This is left for the rough slopes of White Hill and the north ridge to Curleywee. A steep descent from the summit to the Nick of Curleywee leads to Lamachan Hill.

Curleywee can also be reached from the Penkiln Glen by the same forest road that leads to Larg Hill. From Auchinleck in the same glen, an approach can be made by a forest road to Drigmorn where the Pulnee Burn is ascended to the col under Curleywee. An old road crosses this pass to Loch Dee.

## Millfore (656m)

Millfore can be ascended with the three hills to the west in the Lamachan Range, but it is usually taken as an easy day on its own. The approaches are fairly straightforward though they are masked by forests. A car park north of the A712, reached from Craigdews, leads to the west end of Black Loch and a forest road going over a col between Millfore and Poultrybuie Hill. A south-east ridge from there leads to the summit.

On the north side, if the forest road is taken to Loch Dee from Craigencallie, a branch road is taken south at Loch Dee just before an anglers' lodge. This leads on by a firebreak to Cairnbaber and joins the north-east ridge between Cairngarroch (557m) and Millfore.

The finest route to the hill is from the col under Curleywee. The ridge to the east from this col leads past the Black Loch and White Lochan of Drigmorn to the south-west end of the summit ridge where there is a rise at 621m. The White Lochan at 560m was a favourite resort of curlers in the past.

## Cairnsmore of Fleet (711m)

This is the most southerly of the Donalds, almost 90 kilometres south of the Union boundary near Berwick. It is formed of granite and is a paradox of easy grassy meadows and tangled overgrown bristling slopes. It lies east of Newton Stewart and can be approached from a number of directions. The easy route leaves the A75 at Palnure and follows a side road into Cairnsmore estate, rounding some buildings on the north to a car park (472 641). A track north-east across a field leads through the forest to Bardrochwood Moor and an easy climb to the summit where there is a large cairn, a trig point, the ruins of a stone bothy and a granite memorial commemorating eight air crashes involving RAF, USAF and Luftwaffe crews between 1940 and 1979.

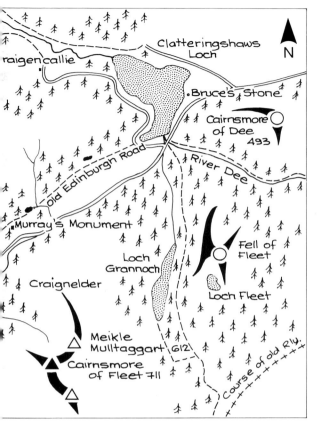

Going south-east from the summit, a fence is joined leading to a col and a wall running across the ridge. Rising ground beyond leads to another large cairn on the Knee of Cairnsmore (656m). A return can be made to the outward path along the ridge, or the Graddoch Burn may be descended to join a forest road going around Crammery Hill.

A long route to the hill starts from the B796 in the south-east. From (546 625) cars may drive as far as the Big Water of Fleet viaduct where a forest road leads on past Meikle Cullendoch to Loch Grannoch. A cairn at the summit of the road above the Cleugh of Eglon commemorates a pony called Maggie. From the edge of the wood at Loch Grannoch the rough slopes of Craigronald lead west then south to Meikle Mulltaggart (612m) and on south-west to Cairnsmore of Fleet.

The hill may also be reached from the A712 at (470 698). A road descends to Corwar and climbs through the forest to (486 688) where a break leads to the Louran Burn and the north-west ridge of Cairnsmore of Fleet. Billy Marshall's Cave is shown on the 1:25,000 map under this ridge. He was a notorious rogue who cared little for authority, but his cave is very hard to find. Another hard-to-find cave on the same hill on the same map is at a head dyke south-west of the summit.

A round from the A712 can include Cairnsmore of Fleet, Meikle Mulltaggart and Craignelder, dropping to cross the Palnure Burn at stepping stones at the caravan park under Murray's Monument. There is a National Nature Reserve east of Cairnsmore of Fleet which visitors are asked to respect.

### Cairnsmore of Dee (493m)
What appears on the map as a short expedition to this hill east of Clatteringshaws Loch should take account of its very rough vegetation on a granite base. A direct approach leads south by a firebreak at a sharp bend on the A712. Farther west another firebreak leads to the north-west spur. There is a trig point and cairn on the summit which is a good viewpoint. The view can be improved by heading west to Benniguinea (387m) and Clatteringshaws Fell, where the walking becomes much easier on a forest trail which descends to join the forest road north of the River Dee.

Criffel from the north

### Criffel (569m)

Despite its modest height, this is a very well known landmark due to its position above the Nith estuary. The most impressive view is from the north where the steep conical form of Knockendoch forms a north ridge to Criffel. A south-west ridge on the hill leads to a col at 430m beyond which there is rough upland walking with less appeal. The hill is easily reached from the A710 south of New Abbey. A side road is taken to Ardwall where cars can be left. A gate to the south leads to a rough road heading for the hill and this route continues up as a firebreak to the heathery corrie north of the summit. The burn from there feeds Loch Kindar which shows several islands. One was built as a crannog. The large Douglas's Cairn is thought to date from the Bronze Age, but takes its name from the powerful earls of the Middle Ages who may have used the hill as a lookout post to defend their territory against the English.

*Burrow Head*

A route to the hill from Kirkbean in the south-east goes through a field behind the houses on the north side of the Kirkbean Glen. A stone-roofed well is passed in the field and a mill dam in the glen, then the edges of the fields lead to the south ridge of Drumburn Hill. Granite boulders litter this hillside and the views can be good to the Solway, England and the Isle of Man. The ridge north from Criffel over Knockendoch gives good views to New Abbey village, its Sweetheart Abbey and the 19th-century Waterloo Monument on the forested slopes across the glen. A descent may be made down the north ridge and a wall followed west through the trees to join a forest road following the Glen Burn to New Abbey.

### Screel Hill (343m)

This hill sits south of Castle Douglas and Gelston and is a popular walk for the superb views it offers over the Solway coast. It is extensively ringed by forestry but is easily reached from the road from the A711 to Gelston. North of Kirkmirran a forest road goes off from a parking area and leads up the east side of the hill before branching south-east and crossing the south-east ridge to the Glen of Screel Burn. A path continues up this glen on to the summit ridge which is rocky and heathery. The cairn is at the west end of this ridge.

### Bengairn (391m)

Forests and electric fences, if not the height, make the traverse of this hill an interesting achievement. It pairs readily with its neighbour Screel Hill for a day out and is, like it, a very good viewpoint. The cols between the two hills were rough enough before they became plantations, but a diversion west along a firebreak is needed now when coming from Screel Hill to gain the north slope of Bengairn. Resourcefulness is required to cross an electric fence on this north slope to gain the summit. The descent from Bengairn to the A711 becomes a long gradual slope past the ruin at Foresthill, but a V-shaped channel between the trees becomes a trap when high electric fences prevent direct access to the road from the west. A road from Greenhill south and west joins with the road from Foresthill and leads to the public road at the north-east end of Bengairn Loch.

## PATHS AND WALKS

*Parton to Creetown.* The former rail route from Dumfries to beyond Glenluce may still be walked for much of its length. The best section lies in the wilds between Loch Ken and the River Cree. The route leaves the vicinity of the A713 at Parton and crosses the Ken by a 'dangerous' bridge to win a way to the west. After Mossdale a fine viaduct leads over the Dee at Stroan Loch and the route climbs to the lonely ruins of a halt at Loch Skerrow. The viaduct at Little Water of Fleet was needlessly blown up by the army, but the impressive Big Water of Fleet viaduct remains and leads back to roads and the descent to the Cree at Creetown. (28 kilometres).

*Clatteringshaws Loch to Loch of the Lowes and A712.* The line of the Old Edinburgh Road starts at the south-west corner of Clatteringshaws Loch and can be followed south-west never more than one and a half kilometres from the A712. The old road was used by Mary Queen of Scots and other monarchs on their visits to Whithorn, but the modern road has been dubbed 'The Queen's Way' for the benefit of tourism. The courses of both routes and the craggy nature of the scenery owe much to glaciation. A forest road takes the old route to its summit past Lillie's Loch under Craignell. A memorial on Darnaw farther north commemorates an airwreck. From Lillie's Loch the route is now a footpath but it joins a forest road again at Black Loch and continues past Loch of the Lowes to turn south-east and join the A712 at (463 692) (12 kilometres).

*Kidsdale to Isle of Whithorn.* From the A747 a signposted road leads to a car park at Kidsdale and access to St Ninian's Cave at Port Castle Bay. The cave is prominent on the north of the bay and was according to tradition the cell occupied by the 4th-century missionary. A splendid cliff walk goes from the south end of the bay to Burrow Head where the scenery is spectacular. The coast lowers as it heads towards Isle of Whithorn and a road out may be joined at Morrach. There is a holiday park behind Burrow Head. Visitors are allowed to park and have access to the cliffs provided they report to the office. (9 kilometres).

*Garlieston to Cruggleton Castle.* This fine walk combines coastal and woodland scenery at the same time and ends on an impressive cliff at the scanty ruins of Cruggleton Castle. The route follows a track south along the coast from Garlieston Harbour and round Rigg Bay. At the end of the wood south of Sliddery Point the path continues along the edge of the field on the cliff edge to the castle. Fences at Palmallet Point try to discourage farther progress south. (5 kilometres).

*Ballantrae to New Luce.* This route leaves the A77 south-east of Ballantrae and becomes a hill track at (115 810) heading south-east over its summit at 424m, only 15m below the summit of Beneraird which is only five minutes away to the north-east. A small cairn between the track and the Main Water of Luce about 400 metres past the col commemorates a gamekeeper who died here. The track splits beyond Lagafater Lodge with a south-east branch going to Glenwhilly to join the New Luce road, and a south-west branch going by Penwhirn Reservoir and the New Luce road or west from the reservoir on a road to Loch Ryan. (25 kilometres).

*The wild goat park above the road at Murray's Monument*

# CROSS-COUNTRY WALKS

## The Southern Upland Way

This 340-kilometre long coast-to-coast footpath crosses the south of Scotland following the south-west to north-east trend of the landscape. The Southern Upland Way is the third official long-distance footpath established in Scotland and crosses the widest reach of the Southern Uplands. It is a challenging route for most walkers, although some athletes have run it in a few days. Most people will require ten days or more at a less hectic pace.

In the west, the route starts at Portpatrick harbour and goes north along the rugged cliff-tops, where there are wide views across the sea to Kintyre, Ireland and the Isle of Man. Secluded coves at Port Mora and Port Kale are negotiated before a road is followed inland from Killantringan Lighthouse on Black Head.

The Rhinns of Galloway are crossed by farm roads and paths by way of Knockquhassen and Ochtrelure, by-passing Stranraer on its southern side and following more minor roads and tracks east of the A716 to Culhorn Mains and Castle Kennedy. This is farming territory with much greenery in the landscape and dairy cattle dotted about the fields. The attractive woodlands, lochs and gardens in the landscaped grounds of Castle Kennedy are seen from the south as the route heads for Chlenry, then the mood changes towards New Luce.

The coastal plain is left behind for the moors and new forests of upland Wigtownshire. Grasses become rougher and cattle hairier, conifers spread across more of the landscape and the ground would be stonier were it not for the large clearance cairns and dry-stone field boundaries which have dealt with the problem.

The scenery is either bleak or compressed by forest beyond Balmurrie, but two standing stones at Laggangarn and the Wells of Rees add historical interest in this remote stretch of countryside before a forest road leads out past Loch Derry to Knowe on the B7027. More forest rides lead to Glenruther and a short cut over Ochiltree Hill brings one to the hamlet of Bargrennan, which is on the bus route between Girvan and Newton Stewart.

The route continues east through the Galloway Forest Park, crossing the Water of Trool at Holm and following the south bank of the river to Caldons Wood, where there is a well-provided camp site. Firebreaks and a forest road lead to a track traversing the slopes south of Loch Trool, where there are splendid views to Glen Trool and Merrick before the sightly sessile oakwoods of Glenhead are passed and a forest trail and road leads up the Glenhead Burn and over a col to Loch Dee.

*Loch Trool*

Here, where it is most needed, is an open bothy at White Laggan, before the forest road leads on to cross the Black Water of Dee and continue to the northern shore of Clatteringshaws Loch and a T-junction east of Mid Garrary. A track is taken up the Pulcagrie Burn to Shield Rig and Clenrie, where a road leads down the Garroch Glen. Beyond Hannaston Wood a path leads over Waterside Hill to Earlstoun Power Station on the A762. Fields are crossed south of this to a footbridge over the Water of Ken and Dalry is entered past the motte.

The Galloway Hills are now left behind, and the Way takes a more northerly course from the east side of Dalry at the top of Main Street. Ardoch and Butterhole Bridge are passed and Culmark Hill crossed, where a fine view may be had of the hills near Carsphairn. The B729 is crossed and the high ground followed east of the Water of Ken by Benbrack and Allan's Cairn to the Chalk Memorial Bothy in the watershed between the Water of Ken and Polskeoch Burn.

The Scaur Water is followed to Polgown, then a path climbs away from the valley round Cloud Hill to drop to Ulzieside, Blackaddie Bridge over the River Nith and an entry to Sanquhar from the south past its castle. The A76 is followed into the town, then Leven Road leads under the railway to a track going north-east straight over a hill to Bog. This is on the line of an old coffin route from Wanlockhead which is followed past Cogshead and over Glengaber Hill to the Wanlock Water, where there are relics of the area's remarkable mining history.

The Way swings to the south-east and climbs to its highest point on Lowther Hill before following the regional boundary fence along the ridge to Comb Head and Laght Hill to the A702 at Over Fingland. This is on a bus route between Edinburgh and Dumfries, though at times it may appear to be as remote as the moon to weary walkers seeking an escape from their task.

The half-way point on the Way is reached at the Potrail Water under Pin Stane and a forest road leads to Daer Reservoir. Beyond the dam the route climbs Sweetshaw Brae to Beld Knowe, passes between Mosshope and the open bothy at Brattleburn and goes east of Rivox to Easter Earshaig and a road to Beattock.

Beyond the Evan Water the walk continues under the A74 and by minor roads to Dumcrieff and a track up the Cornal Burn to Craigbeck Hope and towards the gap between Croft Head and Loch Fell deep in the heart of the Ettrick range. The landscape up there has been afforested and enclosed, but opens out at the col in a surprise view to the rugged Craigmichan Scar. An airy traverse leads above this across the steep slopes of Loch Fell's north-west top to the watershed at Ettrick Head, where a stile leads over into Borders territory and the streams begin to flow towards the North Sea.

An easy descent on a forest road leads down the Ettrick Water past an open bothy at Over Phawhope, and the public road is joined beyond Potburn. The route continues down the road amidst very pleasant scenery to Scabcleuch where the main valley is left and a side valley is followed north towards Peniestone Knowe, Pikestone Rig, Earl's Hill and a descent on an old county road to Tibbie Shiels Inn between the Loch of the Lowes and St Mary's Loch. The south-east bank of the latter is followed past Bowerhope, and the Yarrow Water and A708 are crossed east of Dryhope. Field boundaries lead to an old track near Dryhope Tower and through gaps called the Hawkshaw Doors to cross Douglas Burn at Blackhouse, where another old tower is partly hidden by trees. From Blackhouse a track is taken uphill, going north-east through forest to open slopes across Glenlude Burn and Blake Muir, before dropping to Traquair. Another change of direction leads south-east from there, rising over the northern slopes of Minch Moor to Hare Law and Brown Knowe, and continuing by an old drove road to the very conspicuous cairns of the Three Brethren which mark the meeting of the lands of Selkirk, Yair and Philiphaugh. The Way descends through the forest to Yair to cross the River Tweed by the old bridge on the A707.

*Ettrick Head, a lonely spot on the Southern Upland Way*

A course north-eastwards is now taken from Fairnilee Farm past Calfshaw to round Gala Hill on the southern outskirts of Galashiels and return to the Tweed opposite Abbotsford. The route by the Tweed passes under the A6091 and crosses the Gala Water to join the former Edinburgh to Carlisle railway line to cross over the Tweed to Tweedbank. The line is soon left for a path along the south bank of the river to Melrose, where the Tweed is crossed again by the Chain Suspension Bridge to Gattonside. A brief return is made westwards along the north bank of the river before the Way heads north towards Easter Housebyres and an old track over Kedslie Hill. This route looks directly back to the Eildons, and probably formed part of the Roman Road to the Lothians.

Beyond Bluecairn and Fordswell the Way crosses Woodheads Hill to swing round Chester Hill to Lauder. The Leader Water is crossed in the grounds of Thirlestane castle and a route is followed past Drummonds-hall and Wanton Walls for the last venture into hill country. This is a long stretch through the Lammermuirs by a track to Wheel Burn, then by Scoured Rig and Braidshawrig to the high landmarks of Twinlaw Cairns, from where the North Sea may be seen on a clear

*The Three Brethren*

day. The east ridge of Twin Law leads down to Scarlaw and the road by Rawburn to Longformacus.

There are only low hills to the east now as the Way takes the road from the south end of Longformacus towards Whitchester. A track is followed east past Owl Wood then north to the B6355 at Whitchester Lodge. A northern course is taken along the western edge of Abbey Hill (Outer) above the Whiteadder Water. The river bends to the east and is followed to Abbey St Bathans where a hostel offers overnight accommodation before the final stretch of the Way beyond the river is tackled.

This leads past Whiteburn and Blackburn on tracks and minor roads to drop to the busy A1 and east coast railway line. The road is crossed between the traffic and the railway by a bridge to Penmanshiel Cottage from where an attractive trail leads through Broad Wood and Aikieside Wood to cross the A1107 to Pease Bay. A crush of unscreened caravans at the bay frightens the Way aside to the cliffs above Cove Harbour, which is a tranquil beauty spot with an ancient tunnel through its headland. The cliff-line leads back to the west, and a final kilometre along roads leads to the official end (or starting point) of the Southern Upland Way at the Mercat Cross in Cockburnspath.

## The Forth and Clyde Canal

This 56 kilometre waterway crosses the waist of Scotland between Grangemouth and Bowling. It was opened in 1790 and closed in 1963, but is now gradually being brought back into use for recreation, though sections have been infilled. The towpath on the north bank can be followed from Grangemouth at (905 816) to the Maryhill Junction where the south bank is taken to Bowling by going under the canal. A 500-metre section is infilled at the A82, but the path remains. Alternative finishes can be made into Glasgow by following the branch from Maryhill to Port Dundas or the Kelvin Walkway. The route is well served by public transport.

## The Union Canal

The railway stations at Edinburgh, Linlithgow and Falkirk can divide this 50 kilometre walk into convenient lengths. The canal operated from 1822 to 1965, and has its towpath on the north bank. The Edinburgh end now starts at Fountainbridge. Infilling at Wester Hailes makes a diversion of about one and a half kilometres necessary, and the M8 motorway should be crossed by an overbridge 500 metres to the east and field boundaries followed to regain the route. There are impressive aqueducts at Slateford, and across the Almond and Avon gorges, and a 600 metre long tunnel at Falkirk. The eleven lock descent at the west end of the canal at Falkirk has been filled in, but a road adjacent to the line links with the Forth-Clyde Canal.

## The Antonine Wall

In AD 142 or 143 the Romans constructed this defensive wall stretching 56 kilometres between the Firth of Forth and the River Clyde. The turf ramparts have vanished, but the impressive ditch on the outside can still be followed for much of its length. Good stretches of the Wall can be seen between Falkirk and Kirkintilloch at Watling Lodge (near the west end of the Union Canal), from Rough Castle to Seabegs near Bonnybridge, from Garnhall to Dullatur and over Croy Hill and Barr Hill. The remains of the Wall are easily reached by public transport at many points, and the line of the Wall can be walked in conjunction with sections of the nearby Union and Forth and Clyde canals.

# CLIMBING IN THE SOUTHERN UPLANDS

There are very few high mountain cliffs in the Southern Uplands with climbing potential, the east faces of Craignaw and Dungeon Hill in Galloway being notable exceptions, but there are many small crags, small rocky hills and sea-cliffs which give a good variety of low-level climbing.

Detailed descriptions of many of these crags and the climbs on them are included in the *Climbers' Guide to Central and Southern Scotland*, edited by J.Handren and published by the Scottish Mountaineering Trust (1986). By the end of 1992 this guidebook will be out of print, and a new version entitled *Lowland Outcrops* will be published by the Scottish Mountaineering Club and Trust in 1993. A comprehensive compilation of all the crags in this area, with brief notes about the climbing on them, is available in *The Climbing Guide to Scotland* by T.Prentice, published by the Crowood Press (1992).

Arthur's Seat in Edinburgh has an honoured place in the history of Scottish climbing, Harold Raeburn and his companions having climbed there a hundred years ago. The Salisbury Crags are the longest and most important feature, and there are several other smaller outcrops dotted about the hill,not least of them being Samson's Ribs, which rise directly above the Windy Gowl road near Duddingston Loch. In terms of their fine situation above the city of Edinburgh and the excellent climbing on them, the Salisbury Crags are among the best of Scottish crags. Unfortunately climbing on them is forbidden, but the hope persists that some day this will change and climbers may again be able to enjoy the many splendid little climbs above the capital city.

Traprain Law (OS 1:50,000 Sheet 67, 582 747) is a popular crag for Edinburgh climbers. It is situated six and a half kilometres east of Haddington and those without their own car can reach it by bus, getting off at Overhails Farm on the A1 road. The crags are on the south side of the hill facing the Lammermuir Hills, and there are over 50 routes from Difficult to E1 standard, and of length 5 to 25m.

Ratho Quarry (OS 1:50,000 Sheet 65, 128 709) is the best quarry in the Edinburgh area, and gives a wide range of climbs from Severe to E5 which are considered to be among the best of their type in the south of Scotland. There have recently been fears about the future access to the quarry by climbers, but these appear to have been resolved. Ratho Quarry is reached on foot from the Bridge Inn in Ratho village by the path along the north bank of the Union Canal for just over one kilometre.

Dalmahoy Hill (OS 1:50,000 Sheet 65, 136  671) has a north-facing crag of columnar dolerite, greasy when wet, but pleasantly rough when dry. It gives about 20 routes between Difficult and Hard Very Severe standard of 7 to 25m length. Access is from the A70 road west of Balerno, or from the A71 road to the west of Dalmahoy Country Club.

*Backhill of Bush bothy and the east face of Craignaw*

The Fast Castle sea-cliffs are on the coast between Cockburnspath and Colding-ham, about 60 kilometres east of Edinburgh. Access to them is from the A1107 road five kilometres east of Cockburnspath by a single-track road to Dowlaw Farm, from where paths lead down to the rocky coast. At Fast Castle Head (OS 1:50,000 Sheet 67, 860 711) the foot of the cliffs can be reached by abseil from the bridge at the castle ruins. There are about 12 routes, mostly about Very Severe and upwards, of 45 to 90m length, but the rock is rather poor and the climbs have not become popular.

One kilometre to the east is The Souter (OS 1:50,000 Sheet 67, 868 708), a 20m-high sea-stack. It and the crags around it give good climbing. The Souter has been climbed by a number of routes from Very Severe to E5. The surrounding cliffs, and in particular the two fins of rock immediately north-west of The Souter, give over 30 excellent routes on fine-grained sedimentary rock 8 to 18m high, and of standard Severe to E4. Nesting birds can be a problem during the breeding season (the birds probably think that climbers are also a nuisance) and all the Fast Castle cliffs are best avoided at that time.

A short distance east of The Souter is The Brander, a fine slab facing north-west and jutting out into the sea. There are several excellent 40m routes, Hard Severe to E1, on this slab. To its east there are three other rock fins on which there are more good hard climbs.

Turning to the west, Loudoun Hill (OS 1:50,000 Sheet 71, 609 379) is a little volcanic plug on the north side of the A71 road four kilometres east of Darvel. There is a good selection of routes of all grades up to 45m high on fine rough trachyte on the south-facing crags in a pleasant rural setting.

The Quadrocks (OS 1:50,000 Sheet 63, 220 605) are about one kilometre north-east of Largs on the hillside behind the Inverclyde Centre. There are about 20 routes up to 12m long, most of them in the Very Difficult to Very Severe category. The outlook from the crags across the Firth of Clyde is superb.

In Galloway there are surprisingly few climbing possibilities among the rugged hills of the area. Craigdews (OS 1:50,000 Sheet 77, 497 722) is close to the A712 road, but is in a wild goat park and access is forbidden. On the opposide side of the A712 there are some crags on Craignelder, the northern outlier of Cairnsmore of Fleet. The road which leaves the A712 on the west side of Clatteringshaws Loch ends below Craigencallie (500 783), a clean crag of epidiorite on which there are several routes of 25 to 55m of Very Difficult to E1 standard.

Several kilometres north-west of Craigencallie up the Cooran Lane, and most easily accessible by bicycle along a forest road to Backhill of Bush bothy, are Craignaw and Dungeon Hill (refer to Chapter 15). The east face of Craignaw is a long discontinuous cliff with a classic Very Difficult gully, the central one of three below the summit of the hill.

The east face of Dungeon Hill has a number of crags, of which Cooran Buttress is the most prominent, rising above the Round Loch of the Dungeon. The rock is excellent granite and several fine routes up to 120m long and E2 in standard have been recorded. To the left of Cooran Buttress is the smaller Dungeon Buttress on which a few routes up to E3 have been recorded.

The so-called Dumfries Outcrops include Clifton Crag (909 571), Lion's Head (822 581) and The Thirlstane (993 568). Clifton Crag is a fine south-west facing granite crag with about 50 routes up to 20m long, Difficult to E4. Lion's Head is schist, with six routes from 18 to 32m, and Very Severe to E2 standard. The Thirlstane (Powillimount) is a small sandstone outcrop on the shore near Southerness which gives pleasant climbing from Difficult to E3.

Meikle Ross (OS 1:50,000 Sheet 83, 652 433) is an extensive south-facing array of sea-cliffs on the tip of the peninsula on the west side of Kirkcudbright Bay. The rock is greywacke, a rough hard sandstone. There are over 75 routes of all grades from Difficult to E4 and up to 70m long on the several cliffs which make up Meikle Ross. There is a voluntary ban on climbing on parts of the cliffs from May to August

Burrow Head (OS 1:50,000 Sheet 83, 458 340) is a group of small sea-cliffs on the tip of the peninsula south of Newton Stewart. Access is from the village of Isle of Whithorn past the Burrow Head Caravan Site. The climbs are mostly about 20m long and the standards are from Severe to E3. As on Meikle Ross, there is a moratorium on climbing during the nesting season from May to August.

Laggantalluch Head (OS 1:50,000 Sheet 82, 085 363) is on the west coast of the Mull of Galloway peninsula, about nine kilometres north-west of the Mull. Access is from Kirkmaiden on the B7065 road, reached from the A716 from Stranraer to Drummore.

The excellent granite sea-cliffs give entertaining climbing in pleasant surroundings, with relatively few hazards from sea-birds. The climbs average 15 to 20m, and there is a 40m slab.

The only ice climb of any note in the Southern Uplands, and one that is only rarely in condition, is the Grey Mare's Tail (OS 1:50,000 Sheet 79, 182 150). Access is from the A708 road between Moffat and St Mary's Loch, the start of the climb being a short distance from the road. In conditions of prolonged hard frost this frozen waterfall will give a good 140m climb of Grade III/IV, depending on the quality of the ice and the line taken.

*A solo climber on the first pitch of the Grey Mare's Tail in good winter conditions*

# BIBLIOGRAPHY

Andrew, Ken. *The Southern Upland Way, Vol 1 (west) and Vol 2 (east)*, HMSO, (1984)

Bearhop, D A. *Munro's Tables and Other Tables of Lesser Heights.* Scottish Mountaineering Trust, (1990)

Carter, Paul. *The Forth and Clyde Canal Guidebook.* Strathkelvin District Libraries, (1991)

Crumley, Jim. *Discovering the Pentland Hills.* John Donald Publishers Ltd, (1991)

Drummond, Peter. *Scottish Hill and Mountain Names.* Scottish Mountaineering Trust, (1991)

Forestry Commission. *Forest Park Guide –The Border,* (1958)
                                               *– Galloway,* (1974)

Geikie, Archibald. *The Scenery of Scotland.* MacMillan & Co, (1901)

Grant, Will. *Tweeddale.* Oliver & Boyd, (1948)

Haldane, A R B. *The Drove Roads of Scotland.* Edinburgh University Press, (1971)

Johnstone, Bennet and Brown. *The Corbetts and other Scottish Hills.* Scottish Mountaineering Trust, (1990)

McAdam, A D & Clarkson. E N K. *Lothian Geology – an excursion guide.* Scottish Academic Press, (1986)

McBain J. *The Merrick and the Neighbouring Hills.* Jackson & Sproat, (1980)

McCormick, A. *Galloway: the Spell Of its Hills and Glens.* John Smith & Son Ltd, (1937)

Mack, James Logan. *The Border Line.* Oliver & Boyd, (1926)

Moir, D G. *Scottish Hill Tracks: Old Highways and Drove Roads; 1. Southern Scotland.* Bartholomew & Son Ltd, (1975)

Morris, Albert and Bowman, James. *The Pentlands Pocket Book.* Pentland Associates, (1990)

Natural Environment Research Council (IGS). *British Regional Geology: The South of Scotland.* HMSO, (1971)

Northumberland. *National Park Guide No 7.* HMSO, (1969)

Northumberland National Park. *Walks in Coquetdale,* (1986)
                                               *Walks in the Cheviot Hills,* (1986)

Sissons, J B. *The Evolution of Scotland's Scenery.* Oliver & Boyd, (1967)

Stott, Louis. *The Waterfalls of Scotland.* Aberdeen University Press, (1987)

Williams, David. *A Guide to the Southern Upland Way.* Constable, (1989)

Wright, Gordon & others. *A Guide to Holyrood Park and Arthur's Seat.* Gordon Wright Publishing, (1987)

Yeaman, E J. *Handbook of the Scottish Hills.* Wafaida, (1989)

# INDEX OF PLACE NAMES

LOCAL COLLECTION

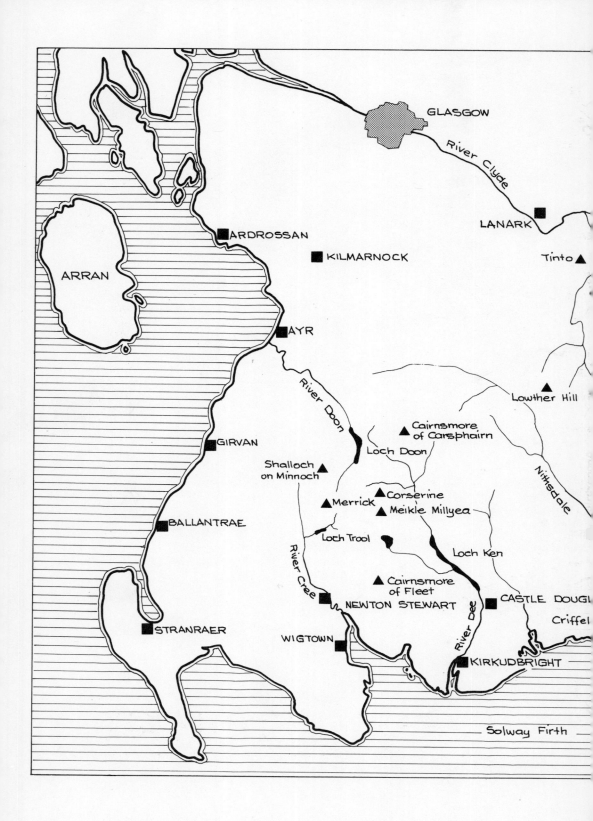